CROOKS AND SQUARES

CROOKS AND SQUARES
Lifestyles of Thieves and Addicts in Comparison to Conventional People

Malin Åkerström

With a Foreword by Donald R. Cressey

Transaction Books
New Brunswick (U.S.A.) and Oxford (U.K.)

Second Printing, 1988
Copyright © 1985 by Transaction, Inc.
New Brunswick, New Jersey 08903

Library of Congress Catalog Number: 85-1199
ISBN: 0-88738-058-1 (cloth)
Printed in the United States of America

Library of Congress Cataloging in Publication Data

Åkerström, Malin
  Crooks and squares.

  Bibliography: p.
  Includes index.
  1. Thieves—Psychology. 2. Deviant behavior. 3. Crime and criminals.
  I. Title.
HV6652.A48   1985   364.3   85-1199
ISBN 0-88738-058-1

4/88

CONTENTS

FOREWORD
Donald R. Cressey

Amateur psychologists, like professional detectives, continue to speculate about the nature of "the criminal mind." Their assumption is that a hidden mental mechanism prompts criminal behavior, and they seem to believe that psychological research eventually will locate it. Those criminologists who are social and behavioral scientists have known for generations that no such mysterious mainspring of action exists. They know, too, that attributing criminality to the workings of an assumed "mind" is a bit like attributing it to devils and demons, neither of which can be observed empirically.

These criminologists have clearly established that criminal behavior patterns (including attitudes) are learned in an observable process involving social interaction and psychological reinforcement. Still, the myth that there is a criminal mind has not been laid to rest, principally because insufficient time and energy have been devoted to conducting and publishing detailed empirical studies of exactly how the learning process works.

The technology for micro-level research on human learning has been developed by those sociologists and linguists calling themselves ethnomethodologists and conversational analysts, but criminologists have not yet made much use of it. Behind this neglect is the fact that criminologists actually know very little about the lifestyles of criminals, including their attitudes about work, leisure, and time as well as their attitudes about law, victims, and crime. Accumulating information about criminal lifestyles is an obvious preliminary to detailed specification of how the many behavior patterns constituting these lifestyles are acquired by individuals.

Crooks and Squares is, thus, an important first step in the long journey to valid scientific knowledge about complex processes which the non-scientific concept of "criminal mind" glosses over. Most exciting, in my view, is the book's documentation of a close resemblance between the attitudes and other behavior patterns of criminals, on the one hand, and the individualistic behavior patterns of entrepreneurs and other capitalists on the other. It is quite possible that professional, organized, and other righteous criminals, at least, have learned the lessons of capitalism too well. Politically speaking, they seem to have learned to think and act like conservatives rather than like liberals or radicals.

The crooks interviewed by Malin Åkerström told her in many indirect ways that they are champions of the ideology of individualism. It is obviously true that if there are only 100 jobs for 200 workers, fifty percent of the workers will be unemployed, no matter what their skills, attitudes, or other personal characteristics. This basic fact is the bedrock of "welfare states" such as Sweden. Yet the author learned that Swedish criminals are not convinced that the simple arithmetic is correct. They, like other advocates of extreme individualism, attribute unemployment and poverty to personal deficiencies such as laziness or poor management of finances. Consistently, they trace their own and others' behavior to personal characteristics rather than to economic, social and political organization. They even look down on people who receive welfare payments.

Moreover, the lifestyle of some of the criminals interviewed by Dr. Akerström is dominated by the criminals' ardent belief in individual freedom and independence - so much so that most cannot even imagine themselves holding down a factory job. The lifestyle also reflects so much enthusiasm for the so-called free-enterprise economic system that the criminals appear to have been personally tutored by Adam Smith. Thus, their behavior documents their conviction that the market place should be goverened by greedy competition. Their conduct also reflects a corollary, namely that rules and regulations which infringe on this form of freedom are questionable at best, even if imposed in the interests of the public good or the general welfare. These criminals do not trust their best friends, let alone their business associates, because they believe that economic rationality, not ethics, governs even personal relationships.

Dr. Akerström's crooks, like many corporation executives, also believe that they can participate in a lifestyle involving extreme individualism without committing crime, a highly doubtful proposition. The ideology of individualism, capitalism, and the market economy have never been predicated on the assumption that people should be free to do whatever they want to generate profits. Some means of making profits have always been outlawed by government officials on the ground that they are unfair to other profit seekers and, thus, to the public at large. Lord Keynes reportedly said that capitalism rests on the almost unfathomable belief that the nastiest of men will, for the basest of motives, work for the benefit of us all. The "nastiest of men," with the "basest of motives" are, of course, those who murder for profit. But even the most enthusiastic supporters of free enterprise do not argue that profit making by such extrem methods contributes to the general welfare. The problem, then, is that of deciding where to draw the line.

Because this problem has yet to be solved, one can easily witness a wide variety of opinions about just what "the rules of the game" of capitalism are, or should be. It is reasonable to believe that most corporation executives, like most ordinary citizens, enthusiastically endorse rules outlawing street-level means of acquiring profits - murder, robbery, burglary, and some varieties of theft. But these same individualists typically deplore criminal laws that limit or control the means by which more genteel entrepreneurs make profits. In the United States, for example, legions of business personnel and government officials are currently convinced that enactment or enforcement of criminal laws outlawing environmental pollution, price fixing, dangerous working conditions, bribery of officials of foreign governments, monopolistic restraint of trade, and the manufacture and distribution of dangerous products is outrageously unpatriotic. Such "socialistic" regulation is unacceptable and must be resisted, these individualists charge, because policing and punishing business and industrial leaders by government agents unjustly interferes with free enterprise. Such resistance, of course, produces high rates of white-collar crime.

But, as noted, individualistic business executives who demand their own freedom from criminal laws and administrative regulations do not ask that this independence be extended to the underprivileged. On the contrary, most of them seem to believe, rather passionately, that the only answer to street crime is strict law enforcement - including certain and severe punishments and, of course, close surveillance. Put another way, they demand that free-enterprise behavior involving stealth, violence and chicanery by working-class people, but not by themselves, be tightly restricted by government regulators.

It is reasonable to assume that not all young, male, poor central-city dwellers are interested in - or even capable of - drawing this fine line between what is acceptable and what is not acceptable free-enterprise behavior. *Crooks and Squares* suggests that a minority of them - those who wind up in prison - have taken a rather pure form of the ideology of individualism to their bosoms. This ideology, championed by capitalists, encourages each citizen to disregard social welfare and to maximize personal selfish satisfactions. Achievement of economic success is considered a sign of moral worth. It follows that laws and rules of ethics which interfere with such achievement are not to be obeyed unthinkingly. They are relevant to the governance of one's personal competitive conduct only to the degree that one believes they do not unjustly interfere with free enterprise, independence, and personal freedom. Accordingly, some laws are to be violated as a matter of principle.

Sooner or later, working-class people who have learned to base their lifestyle on these cherished beliefs are bound to be arrested.

INTRODUCTION

"It's not society's fault that I'm a criminal. I'm in it for the money," stated a thief during one of my first interviews. A drug addict told me that it wasn't the drugs that made him return to "the life" but the lifestyle surrounding it - the thrills, the company and the business. Statements such as these seemed to counter a lot of criminological theory and aroused my interest in criminal lifestyles outside prisons: which elements are exciting and which are dull? What are the problems, and the strategies for solving them? Are social workers 'more trouble than they're worth'? Are they there just to be duped and taken advantage of?

Several scholars have pointed out that we know relatively little about crime as a way of life.[1] Most of our research and theories deal with the causes of crime and of becoming a criminal. It is equally important however to discover how such groups actually perceive, assess and deal with their situation. Studies of this type have centered mainly around drug addicts, while my primary interest is property criminals-robbers, thieves, etc. Previous research about these criminals dealt mainly with crime as work,[2] whereas I felt it necessary to cover a broader spectrum and take up more aspects of their lives.

Seeking answers to questions such as 'what are the pro's and con's of a criminal lifestyle in comparison with a more conventional one' helps us to enrich our knowledge about the everyday life of criminals. But more important, these questions themselves must be brought to the fore in order to understand the causes for becoming and remaining a criminal.

Matza (1969), a well-known criminologist, has argued that we need these types of studies, made with an attitude of 'appreciation', in order to understand the individual's world as it appears to him. This 'appreciation' makes a qualitative method almost a necessity. Even though I have used both quantitative and qualitative material, the latter have thus inspired me more because of my assumption that human beings are quite competent social actors. Lofland has expressed the correlation between this theoretical view and qualitative method in the following way: "... qualitative strategy analysis seeks to increase ranges of **action options** engaged in by people in situations regardless of their frequency of correlation... In a sense, qualitative strategy is the empirical codification of social action wisdom. If people... under study emerge as superstrategies and supersophisticated, this is fitting." (1976:71-72)

Most authors analyze or describe a criminal group as a 'subculture', emphasizing the norms and values of this subgroup. I work rather with the concept 'lifestyle'[3], stressing instead the activities that are valued by the actors.

The fact that lifestyles are shared gives rise, of course, to shared vocabularies of meaning, values, norms and perspectives and thus to subcultures. The criminal or addict subculture should not however be seen as too embracing or coercive.[4] I have wanted to avoid a cultural deterministic view of the actors. Most criminals have led other, more conventional types of lives as well and few foresee their future dedicated to a career of crime.[5] A criminal or addict lifestyle is thus often a temporary one and was perceived as such by the interviewed persons.

Lifestyle as a concept is also useful since it allows for an understanding of how actions and norms are situationally motivated; i.e., an actor's way of life limits certain options while it allows for others. The discovery that thieves tend to be spendthrifts, for example, was explained by several rational factors. They have few formal ways of saving open to them since the authorities would want to know how they got hold of their money. Subcultural analysis, on the other hand, has explained their tendency to spend by simply stating that hedonism is part of their culture. It is thus important to keep in mind the specific circumstances surrounding the demands on and opportunities for criminals. Thus, Goffman's work has been used extensively due to his emphasis on social actors, their strategies and 'situational demands'.

Thus, in much of my analysis I have tried to make actions and norms of criminals intelligible from the viewpoint of their instrumental value. For a full understanding of a group, however, actions, norms and identities are of course important in their own right. 'Spendthriftiness' for example can naturally not only be seen as an instrumental way of adjusting to a situation but also can reflect an ideological position which is directed against what is seen as a dull, cautious conventional society. Furthermore, thieves' emphasis on individual responsibility is important - especially since it counters the common view in criminological texts. Likewise, the respondents' inclination to view themselves as businessmen has of course bearing on their actions, apart from also giving us a somewhat different definition of crime as such.

Finally, I believe that in much of latter-day criminological analysis, the fact that activities should be seen as rewarding to some degree in order for people to be attracted enough to continue with them is neglected. One scholar expresses for example the differences between the earlier, classical research by Thrasher from the Chicago school and that of the later subcultural analysis in the following manner:

Thrasher's boys enjoyed themselves being chased by the police, shooting dice, skipping school, rolling drunks. - Cohen's boys and Cloward and Ohlin's boys are driven by grim economic and psychic necessity into rebellion. It seems peculiar that modern analysts have stopped assuming that 'evil' can be fun and see gang delinquency as arising only when boys are driven away from 'good'. (Bordua, 1961:136)

The present work was initially conceived as a result of the contrast between my initial stereotype of the criminal as a grey, depressed, dreary person - a stereotype influenced a great deal by the recent criminological literature - and the reality of the real, living criminal which I later gained through interviewing them.

These criminals impressed me with their self-confidence, resourcefulness and ability to describe their situation - often in a humorous way, which I hope I have been able to do justice to and communicate in the present work.

1
METHOD AND SAMPLES

This work is based upon three different empirical studies of Swedish male prison inmates who have committed crimes against property or drug laws. The first, (Persson 1977)*, concerned aspects of the illegal market. It consisted mainly of taped interviews with male inmates and policemen. The second study (Persson 1978) consisted of some informal interviews as well as interviews through questionnaires to one hundred and one inmates. The research topics dealt with attitudes towards drugs, different types of legal jobs, illegal ways of supporting oneself, opinions of the "square-johns" and about crime as a way of life for thieves and addicts respectively.

The third study was carried out in 1981, using the same methods as earlier. The questionnaire this time was, however, a bit more extensive, and I took more care in trying to get as many inmates as possible in nine prisons to participate. I enhanced the interview itself by announcing beforehand that all interviewees would be given coffee, cakes and cigarettes while filling in the questionnaire. Furthermore, the inmates at most prisons were

* Previous publications have been made in my maiden name, Persson.

permitted to do this during their work-hours without any reduction of their daily pay. The arrangements around the interviews seemed to be quite effective, since very few of the inmates refused. The only ones who did not participate in eight prisons were either a few who refused or those who were sick at the time, had visitors or were on leave. At one prison I was not allowed to assemble the inmates for the interview. Therefore, I distributed the questionnaires and came back a few days later to collect them. When I returned, some said they had forgotten the whole thing, some had mislaid them, etc. About a fourth of those to whom I had given the questionnaire at this prison did not give them back. Furthermore, on one of the wards, all the inmates refused to fill it in. I had not been able to distribute the questionnaires myself on that particular ward. The prison guard who passed them out did it quite clumsily: he told the inmates to line up, and more or less ordered them to take the questionnaire - which they refused. I managed, however, to make a deal with them by settling for taped interviews. This turned out to be better, in fact, because these inmates were all considered as "reliable guys" or "right guys" by other inmates. Most of them belonged to what I have called the "traditional thieves" - the group I was most interested in. Thus, in these informal talks, I got a great deal more information, I think, than I would have gotten otherwise. All in all, one hundred and fifty inmates, from nine prisons, are included in the questionnaire study. In addition, a total of fifty taped interviews were conducted.

In order to compare the answers from the inmates, I used two different non-criminal samples. First I was kindly allowed by Professor Hans Zetterberg to use his original data file for a nationwide study made by SIFO (The Swedish Institute of Public Opinion Research). I matched the respondents so that they were of the same age as the inmates and, of course, only men were selected. This sample is referred to as **SIFO.**

Furthermore, I collected a comparison group from a sample of white-collar and blue-collar male workers at a factory, Alfa-Laval, in Lund, Sweden. I tried to match these with the inmates according to age, but they are, on the average, a bit older than the inmates. The blue-collar workers were mostly mechanics. The white-collar workers were engineers, economists or salesmen. With the support of the company management and the labor unions, the chosen interviewees were asked to fill out a questionnaire and mail it back to me. Considering the method used here, the amount who actually answered and sent back their questionnaires, 73%, must be seen as satisfactory. This group is referred to as **"control group"** in the tables and in the text. The social classification, age, status and education of the different groups are shown in Tables 1-4.

Apart from the interviews mentioned above, I used tape recorded interviews with other conventional groups made in conjunction with studies of leisure and consumption. Furthermore I have become acquainted with some ex-thieves and ex-addicts, who shared their experiences with me. And finally, as in Shover's (1971) study of burglars, this work also benefited from a range of biographies and autobiographies of criminals.

General characteristics of my data

My intention in making this study has been to analyze some essential features in criminals' lifestyles outside prison. In order to accomplish this, I had to get access to a criminal group as well as a non-criminal group. Time, money and obvious research-technical reasons have, however, made it impossible to find groups that can somehow be seen as representative. My criminal group, for example, is characterized by its being imprisoned at the time of the study, which obviously implies an over-representation of criminals who get caught as compared to a random sample of all criminals, as has been shown that "able criminals" spend less time in prison.[1] In a similar fashion, one can argue that employees at one factory are not necessarily representative of ordinary Swedish men.

I do believe, however, that the discussions and conclusions concerning similarities and differences between the groups would not have differed very much had the groups been selected in a different way.

The different criminal groups

On the basis of my previous experiences in earlier studies, I decided in my third study to divide the inmates according to the categories they used themselves: "thieves" and "addicts". These categories seemed more applicable than, for example, a differentiation based upon different offenses. Very few were specialized in only one type of criminal act: the general concensus among them was that one had to be a jack-of-all-trades today to make it.

To be a thief, then, does not mean only to be specialized in stealing. The concept was used by the inmates as meaning a criminal in a wider sense, as someone who mostly supports himself by crime in general and who identifies himself and is identified by others in his group as a "thief". Addicts on the other hand were those who were involved in crime because of drugs. If drugs were seen as their main motivation, they were labelled addicts whether they stole or not.

I found, however, that these two groups were not sufficient when I tried to divide the respondents into one or the other, since many landed in between. I therefore constructed two more groups, "modern thieves" (as opposed to the orginal category, now termed "traditional thieves") and "mixed".

At first, I tried to select a few items from the questionnaire and make the differentiation by computer-analysis. I soon discarded this method, as some of the respondents did not answer the key questions essential to making the divisions. Furthermore, given the human element of individuality, some of the inmates' answers could not be codified into previously-determined groupings, as "ideal types" often do not exist in reality. I therefore decided to do this work manually and on qualitative grounds. The main items I used were questions concerning their self-identity, if they were drawn into crime due to drugs or not, attitudes towards addicts, whom they preferred to associate with, their main reason for committing crime, and if they viewed their lifestyle in a positive or negative way. If I was still uncertain - some cases were of course difficult to place - I had additional help from remarks written in the margin or on the back of the questionnaire, and from other questions that I saw as clues to their identity.

Traditional thieves

This group consists of those who, more often than the others, described themselves as thieves or as criminals. They saw positive features in their lifestyle, and many described themselves as professional thieves who had chosen their way of living themselves. Fifteen of the forty-one who make up this group stated that they had never tried drugs. Even those who had tried - a few had even been addicted - were nevertheless, very negative towards addicts. This group is also a bit older than the others.

Modern thieves

This category consists of people who have described themselves as thieves, or stated that they are thieves and drug users. This group is not negative towards addicts. Only two of the fifty who belong to this group stated that they had never tried drugs. Thirty of them had tried three or more different types of drugs. They associate with addicts as well as with thieves. Their own addiction, however, was not given as the primary cause for their criminality. Crime or drug-dealing was often seen as a business enterprise by this group. One respondent said for example, "My granddad was a horse dealer, my dad, a car dealer, and I, myself, am a drug dealer." It can be added that he supplemented his income with thefts of various kinds. This group is younger than the rest. Maybe these are tomorrow's typical "thief" who is engaged in thefts as well as drug-dealing (assuming that this will continue to be a lucrative business).

Mixed

This group resembles the "disorganized criminal", as described by Gibbons, Roebuck and Johnson, and Irwin. They do not, as the previous group, find the same attraction to a life of crime, and they are not as committed to such a life as criminals like those above. They do not speak about having chosen their life, and seem to look at themselves as losers. Only one of the twenty-one who belong to this category had not tried drugs. Fifteen had tried three or more different types of drugs. They do not, however, identify themselves as addicts, but as people who are drug users and thieves because of personal problems.

Addicts

The nineteen in this group that I have called "addicts" have all stated that they have been or are addicted to different types of drugs (it should be remembered that they are presently in prison, therefore the "have been"). The basis for my categorization here is the fact that all of them stated that they had committed crime because of their drug dependancy. They saw their addiction **per se** as the reason for their criminality; several of them stated that if drugs had been legal, they would not have been in prison. Some also argued that they were not "really criminals". Their description of themselves was "addict", "drug user", or something else like "an artist of life" or "seeker of the truth". They preferred to associate with addicts or drug users rather than with thieves.

In addition to the respondents categorized as above, there were some that I put in an "other" group. They were all special in some way: some had converted to religious beliefs in prison that made them deviate from the others. There were also some forgers from a more middle-class background than the rest of the interviewees. Since they had committed crimes against property, I did not sort them out entirely.

Problems in interviewing

In a study of this kind, it is of obvious importance how the interviewer-researcher is looked upon by the respondents. I tried to present myself as a researcher first, but also as an outsider who was interested in being taught by the respondents about their lives - an area where they were the experts, and I, the pupil. At the same time, I tried to avoid being "too hip", something Irwin (1972) warns students of deviants against. I would rather put myself in the role of the dumb, "not-in-the-know" outsider, and in this manner get information and statements about problems or issues where I was insecure of my knowledge. Further, this approach gives the respondent somewhat of an upper-hand during the interview, which allows him to feel that his information is interesting and valuable.

Another important issue is where the interview are carried out. Polsky (1969) has argued that in order to get an accurate picture when studying criminals, one has to use participant observation. To study them in institutions is said to be comparable to studying animals in cages. Apart from participant observation not being practically possible, there are actually advantages in doing interviews in prison. As Agar (1980) points out when comparing a study he did with addicts at a treatment home and addicts in the street, the former informants were better because they had more time to reflect and think about the questions. The addicts in the streets were difficult to talk to because their attention was elsewhere, revolving around their present and/or future deals and businesses, they were difficult to "catch and keep" long enough to be interviewed, and in addition, they were often high on drugs. To live with them and do real participant observation was often not allowed since by nature their activities were secret and they wanted to protect themselves. This problem is something I undoubtedly would have encountered.

It can also be added that Shover (1972) who studied burglars reports that interviewing them outside or inside prison did not have any differentiating impact.

Generally, I think the bias of the environment of prison would be less in this type of study - analyzing the lifestyle, work, etc. - than if one were asking inmates about prison-related areas such as attitudes towards punishment and treatment-orientated problems.

Table 1. Social classification according to the Swedish Central Bureau of Statistics' "socioeconomic division", 1980.

%	Non-vocationally trained worker	Vocationally trained worker	White-collar worker			Own firm	Farmer or House-whife	No answer	Sum	N
			low	middle	high					
Father's social group:										
Inmates	31	21	7	6	4	14	3	15	100	(150)
Blue-collar worker	20	24	7	18	7	5	13	7	100	(105)
White-collar worker	11	24	11	20	11	5	15	2	100	(93)
Mother's social group:										
Inmates	33	7	9	9	1	2	23	17	100	(150)
Blue-collar worker	20	5	12	8	2	2	44	8	100	(105)
White-collar worker	19	3	9	13	2	2	48	3	100	(93)

Table 2.

%	Age 17-24	25-34	35-	Sum	N
Inmates	42	39	19	100	(150)
Control group	28	54	18	100	(198)

Table 3.

%	Status Married/ cohabiting	Girl friend	Divor- ced	Single	No answer
Inmates	21	31	17	29	3
Control group	56	14	4	26	-

Table 4.

%	Completed level of education Primary school	Vocational school or 2-year secondary school	Other	Univer- sity
Inmates	50	26	23	-
Blue-collar workers	11	47	39	3
White-collar workers	1	10	37	53

2
CRIME AS WORK

Several criminologists have analyzed crime as work. Sutherland portrayed in a classical book, *The Professional Thief*, the life and work of professional thieves and con men. Maurer, a linguistic scholar, concentrated on con men in *The Big Con* and *The Wiz Mob*. Polsky (1969) wrote about pool hustlers and their work situation and pointed out the lack of analysis continuing in the tradition of Sutherland's study, since research had become concentrated around the causes of crime. Lately, however, the older tradition has returned to favor. Klockars has made an excellent study of *The Professional Fence*, Shover studied "good burglars" in his dissertation *Burglary as an Occupation* and Letkemann concentrated on work methods of robbers and safe-crackers in *Crime as Work*. Finally, I would like to mention Prus and Sharper's account of the careers of professional card and dice hustlers in *Road Hustler*.

Common for all these studies is that they emphasize how criminals live and work instead of why criminals are what they are. This perspective allows them to avoid grand theories and half-hidden value judgements.[1] Analyzing crime as work seems to imply a more articulated description and understanding of the life and work of different criminal groups.

I am not going to give a detailed account of crime as work in the common terms of career processes, work methods, etc., here. Instead, I will examine whether the criminals themselves tend to look at their activities as work and what special skills and problems they indicate are connected with supporting oneself by crime. Thereafter it will be argued that earning one's income by illegal means demands a lot of individual initiative and creativity. Finally, it is concluded that the skills and time used in making necessary connections and so on can be seen as an investment by the criminals as in any other types of work.

Crime as work?

"Crime as work?"
"Yeah, I guess you could look at it that way ... I hope no worker will listen to this." (laughter)

The interviewees define their way of supporting themselves as both work and non-work. They regard it as work in the sense that it does involve skills, physical activities and strain but at the same time, they do not define crime as "an occupation". Furthermore, they often point out that the whole meaning of being a criminal is to avoid "work".

Miller has used the housewife and the members of Hare Krishna as examples of people doing work but not having an occupation. He discusses the differentiation between these concepts in the following way:

Work is defined as the various ways in which human beings attain their livelihoods ... Occupation is a unique type of work role based on two factors: (1) its existence as a role discrete and separate from the other roles occupied by the individual, and (2) the primary use of such direct financial rewards as salaries or wages to obtain a minimal level of involvment in the role by the worker. (1980:382)

Criminals' ways of supporting themselves illegally can be looked at in the same way. They themselves seem to define their work along this line. Although the respondents seldom talked about thievery as an occupation, they referred to break-ins as "jobs" or that they "went working".

An example of how stealing can be seen as work is given by a "modern thief" who referred to this in the following casual way:

> When you didn't have money for drugs you'd usually go out after two at night and work. Between two and six I used to steal and after that go down to the fence with my stuff.

He also claimed that he was too lazy "to work" but corrected himself immediately:

> Well, it's not really laziness because you work twice as much as other people. Take, for example, driving a car for 24 hours: you have to drive carefully so that nothing will happen. So you do work. It's not that kind of laziness, but you want to do something for yourself.

Since many had talked about crime requiring a lot of effort and that it was "hard work" both in a physical and psychological sense, I posed the following statement in the questionnaire: "It requires more hard work to support oneself as a thief than by ordinary work." It is interesting that it was mostly those who have experience in this who agreed, half of the thieves, compared to only a third of the mixed and the addicts. Some thieves referred to stress in the taped interviews, caused by having to work under extremely uncertain conditions with an unsure outcome, often with rather unreliable partners, and with the unpleasant prospect of being arrested. The "easy buck" is thus not all that easy. So why do they continue? The answer seems to be that the costs are worth it as long as the alternative of ordinary work is considered worse.[2]

Specialization or being a jack-of-all-trades?

Several scholars have noted a decline in the specialization of professional criminals.[3] This is said to be caused by increased technical difficulties - better safes, non-cash money transfers, etc. For some criminals this development has probably led to what McIntosh (1971)labels "project crimes" with much planning and investment beforehand and where the stakes are high, instead of what she called the craft-crimes, for example, what safe-crackers were involved in before. For most criminals, however, even those who call themselves professionals as Gould (1968) has noted, hustling is a more common practice. Hustling refers to constantly being on the outlook for every opportunity, for example moving around bars finding out "what's up", and "connecting" on a less planned basis with others for fencing, stealing, drug deals, etc. The interviewees confirmed that there was indeed a need today to constantly be on the outlook for "angles to make a buck". One man, for example, made the following rather typical comment:

"You can't live on thieving, you have to combine it with being a businessmen, sort of."
"Is everyone doing that?"
"Yeah, I think so, ya gotta cut your coat according to your cloth ... Thieves committing perfect crimes, as they say, that's something I don't believe in. Maybe in the old days when they went out on a bike and blew safes, but the times have changed..."

He thus seems to agree to specialization being more common before. It is however difficult to know whether this is right or not. Reading older biographies of criminals you get the impression that being a "jack-of-all-trades" has always been a necessity. The following is an account from thirty years ago:

So you see, there was a lot of ways to make a
dollar ... A lot of people think that once a
stickup man, always a stickup man. Well, you can't
run around stickin' up people every day of the
week like a workin' man. (Martin, 1952:117)

Most criminals not only resort to a variety of
crimes but also add to their incomes different legal
means of support. Most in my study had relied on
legitimate work, sick leave benefits, unemployment
compensation, and so on for a good part of their
earnings. Holzman's (1979) study of robbers and
burglars reports the same overall tendency. He
concludes that their criminal activities follow a
secondary rather than primary source of income and
actually describes his subjects as "moonshining in
crime". However, he also reports that most burglars
do not rob and robbers do not commit burglary to a
high extent. They thus have, as Letkemann's (1973)
interviews with property offenders also indicate, "a
line". Having "a line" rather than being totally
professionally specialized is I think the reason for
the rather interesting results I got when I asked my
interviewees whether they were mainly specialized
and what they thought other thieves were.

Table 5.

%	I	Others
Commit many types of crime	40	89
Am/Are specialized	60	11
N	(117)	(132)

The results indicate both a feeling that one has a
speciality (even if one has to do other things to
support oneself) and also that this is a form of
identity. At the same time they see others doing a
lot of different things in order to get by
financially and therefore downgrade the criminal
community's degree of specialization as compared to
themselves. However, the result does not indicate,

as one could believe, that claiming a specialization is a matter of status-seeking. At least not to the respondents, since three-fourths denied in answer to another question that being specialized was something that gave criminal status and respect.

Skills

When it comes to skills in this type of work the respondents very rarely mentioned specialized mechanical skills[4] as an important factor in supporting oneself by crime. Instead they pointed out some special conditions such as that it demands nerve, coolness and the ability to make connections.

The importance of having courage

Craftmanship was thus not considered important but having "guts" was seen as a more vital factor. Some even felt that this was something you had to be born with! A common statement was that, "most people could never take it", i.e., the dangers and risks inherent in the criminal lifestyle. This aspect was also important in choosing associates, since someone who was scared could not be trusted.

> There are some guys who're scared and I tell 'em: if you can't take it, tell me now, it's worse later - then it might be too late. And a guy like that who can't keep his nerve, he'll put me in a spot, not only himself, you know.

However, as Shover (1971) and West (1974) have pointed out, **too** much nerve can also be bad since it can lead to carelessness. A combination of having "guts" and being cool is thus the ideal. A safe-cracker states that now, after several years of criminal life, he is never afraid:

> You learn how to master both your nerves and your feelings, to think coldly. A person who loses his cool, he's totally unpredictable and could do

absolutely anything. But someone who's calm and
doesn't think too much but just does what he's
doing at the moment, he can react afterwards and
he's much more effective.

Shover also points out the fact that losing one's
nerve can sometimes be the reason for quitting at
least those criminal activities where courage is
needed. Some of my respondents also mentioned that
some burglars they knew had quit because of this.
One former thief agreed that though he had no
scruples about committing a crime, he would be too
scared nowadays to do so.

Even though taking drugs before committing a crime
was not recommended (those who considered themselves
good stated that they did not use drugs before a
job), quite a few used either narcotics or alcohol
in order to get the needed confidence or courage. Of
those who were influenced by drugs, and who
commented on why they had used them, some gave
answers like "in order to stay calm". (This is of
course contrary to those who take drugs for no
special criminal purpose and then, "after you take
something, you do stupid things".) One can thus
conclude that since courage is such an important
aspect, it will lead at least some criminals to use
drugs before they commit crimes.

Coolness

Coolness is related to having courage, but still is
not the same - you can be brave yet "blow your
cool". Coolness according to Irwin has two
dimensions:
First is the ability to keep one's composure in
the face of difficulties encountered on capers...
Second, coolness is involved in the day-to-day
living of the thief. The good thief lives in an
unobtrusive manner, careful not to draw unwanted
attention and "heat". (1970:9-10)
Coolness is not only required, it is also a valued
trait, giving status to those who possess it.

"Someone who is calm and cool in all situations" was the most common answer (31% checked it off) to the question "Who is especially appreciated and respected outside the joint by other criminals?"[5] This may be part of the answer to why the demand for coolness can win over the demand for loyalty in the in-group. A liquor-store owner in one of the rougher areas of San Fransisco told me about a man who had been stupid enough to try to break into a police car. Soon afterwards another man in the area came in, a known drug dealer, and told the store-owner who had done it. Bill, the owner, promised not to reveal who the "snitcher" was. When the police came to the store to ask him if he knew anything about the attempted break-in, Bill passed on the information, while being assured in his turn that the source of information would not be revealed. When I asked him why the first man had told him, Bill responded, "The guys down here thought it was a stupid thing to do, they don't want any heat down here."

Coolness is however not only a required skill and a valued trait; it is also a state-of-being, one which can be enjoyed for its own sake, even if foolheartedly. This state is often enchanced through drugs. One former addict told me that when high on heroin, he loved flirting with danger:

> The good thing about heroin, you see, is that it makes you so cool. You can walk into, say, a jewelry store in the middle of the day and steal right in front of them and then you walk away before they have time to call the police ... It's great ...

Making connections

Contacts are essential to the criminal in several ways, both for his criminal pursuits and for his overall living pattern. Contrary to the picture of young addicts being dragged into drug-using circles, they have to work to gain access to these groups.

... the world of young drug users, operates as a selective device, indicating the kind of youngsters who will be accepted at one point or another and by the same token, the kind of person who will be denied access to drugs. (Blumer et al, 1967:48)

Even if you are known in an area, it is not easy to buy from someone in the street. You must prove yourself trustworthy. In Pryce's study of West Indian lifestyles in England, one group is labelled "inbetweeners" - those inbetween the law-abiders and the hustlers. If someone from this group wants to get hold of marijuana, he has to get acquainted with the hustler group:

Of course, procurring marijuana is not just simply a matter of exchanging cash for the stuff. In order to obtain 'a smoke' in Shanty Town, the inbetweener, not being a hustler himself, must become affiliated with hustlers, learn their values and norms, and become acquainted with the dealers. (1979:248)

To reach the higher echelons in the drug-dealing world is of course even more difficult. Consider, for example, the difficulties involved in making contact with this described dealer:

The most secretive tactic is to **avoid meeting any new people.** One dealer, in the business for a dozen years, refuses to go anywhere he might encounter someone unknown. He will sit outside in his car rather than chance seeing someone who does not know him. (Adler and Adler, 1980:454)

The problems of maintaining the necessary balance between social openness and closedness in the criminal world is even shown in the area of prostitution. According to Prus and Vassilikopoulos (1979), it is not even self-evident that every customer with money "scores", since street-walkers also have other gate-keeping requirements. Thus, even in this context, the easy access that is often assumed is not always present. The element of secrecy within criminality is one of the problems that the aspiring burglar must cope with when trying to gain access to rather closed social circles:

If the fledgeling burglar is to progress and

become proficient and succesful in his endeavors, he must gain entrance into a closed social circle. He must establish relationships with those kinds of people who can teach him and assist him in coping with the problems endemic to burglary. (Shover, 1972:542)

Even after having gained the trust of fellow burglars, the problem of selling may remain. Since buyers of stolen goods do not advertise openly and since having a fence is often a prerequisite for stealing, it is very important to acquire one. This information is not easily attained:

"Do thieves sell to each other?"
"Yeah, sure, there's always some thief who knows someone who is not a thief and who is looking for something."
"Doesn't everyone know a fence or someone like that?"
"No, no, only some do. Say that there are fifty quite well-established thieves in Malmö, only thirty of those have a fence. Those who don't are the younger ones around eighteen or twenty who haven't been around enough, so they'll have to ask their friends or sell to thieves. For someone who's been inside as much as me, it's no problem."
"Would you tell a young guy who's buying?"
"No way. I wouldn't do that. But I could say 'What do you have?' And he'd say, 'I have some gold,' because that's what's common... 'Well, if you dare put it in my hands, I'll keep it for you. But then you'll have to stay here in my apartment until I come back.' Because he won't be allowed to come along because I don't want to show him who I'm selling to."

It is no wonder then that a young thief said that one has to track like the Indians to find the fences, and dog the steps of one's associates. Someone else told me about how he had established a contact with a gasoline station owner:

I was with a friend and he sold a stereo to this
guy. So when I had a little car stereo and really
needed money, I thought, 'Do I dare go out to that
guy who owns the gas station? Yeah, I'll take the
chance and go out there.' 'Hi, we were here a
couple of days ago and sold a stereo. Would you
like to buy this one as well?' He looked at me a
bit suspiciously and asked who I was with. 'So and
so.' 'Yeah, that's right. I'll take a look at it.'
And that's how I got that contact.

Practical knowledge

A more general comment on crime as work is that even
though criminals may not need specialized
craftmanship, they do need a lot of practical
knowledge: how to break into a house or a store, how
to handle people, how to judge potential buyers. If
selling, they have to know what they are dealing
with, so as for example not to sell white gold as
silver out of ignorance, a situation that one fence
gladly took advantage of.[6] Similarily a drug dealer,
for his own sake, should be personally acquainted
with the drugs he sells. Some of the business-minded
thieves had actually tried various drugs for this
reason after deciding to go into this branch. The
reason for this type of knowledge being so important
in the criminal world is of course the lack of pro-
tective institutions, like the Governmental
Department for Consumer Affairs or the Consumer
Ombudsman, which one can turn to if cheated.[7]

Practical knowledge as referred to here does not
only apply to knowledge about things, language, etc.
but also to knowledge about people. The lack of
traditional sources of information such as grades,
employment certificates, company magazines, etc.,
makes it vital in the criminal world to acquire
knowledge about people. The grapevine is said to
travel fast in these circles:

"You know rather a lot about each other in this
world?"

"Yeah, before you do business, you get information
on guys. And then you hear you should avoid this
one and that one, it travels fast."

Illustratively the famous British train robbers who
successfully fled to Mexico had problems in taking
up their old profession again because "... they
concluded quite quickly that without criminal
contacts or a good knowledge of the language it
would be futile." (Read, 1979:257)

Making a living through crime requires a lot of
individual decision-making, judgement and knowledge
about a wide range of things, often more than in
non-criminal pursuits, characterized by
specialization. The type of knowledge, however, can
differ: Sowell (1980) has pointed out that knowledge
today is often associated with theoretical and
reasoning skills. This is also considered the
superior type. He therefore wants to emphasize the
existence and importance of "authentication of
knowledge", i.e. the ability to implement in a
practical way a project or task, not just
theoretically knowing how. He also notes that the
members of lower strata of society in general need
comparatively more practical knowledge than other
groups in order to make it in the world.

Crime as creativity

Criminals are commonly portrayed as leading more or
less passive lives, led or driven by fate and
circumstance. To the contrary, their lifestyles
require a lot of inventiveness and active work.

The element of creativity in criminal work

I was often impressed with the creativity the
respondents showed in supporting themselves. One
aspect of this is the ability of property criminals
to view everyday surroundings - buildings, situations - in the light of crime potential. Lofland
sees this ability among criminals to reshuffle

elements as creativity, a kind of innovation:

The more conventional sort of creativity and the present type also occur under similar circumstances: a stressful situation which demands a reconceiving of the cognitive field in order to achieve a solution... And, as with other discoveries of new possiblities for action or meaning, once they are known, others are likely to say, "It is so obvious" or "it was so easy". (1969:73)

Creativity is also required in the learning process. First of all, in Sweden criminals are not brought up in particularly criminal neighborhoods where skills are picked up and contacts made. Thrasher's study of "the gang" from the twenties in Chicago describes a taken-for-granted reality of crime. The experiences of the gangland boys then and there differ quite a lot from those of the persons interviewed in this study:

Most adolescent gangs have an intimate knowledge of the doings of the underworld... The gang boys sees lawlessness everywhere and in the absence of effective definitions to the contrary accepts it without criticism. He soon learns where to buy stills, skeleton keys, and guns, which are sold to minors with impunity, either by mail or by dealers who have them on open display. (1966:186, new ed.)

Secondly, the way thieves learn their work has often been described as a tutelage process, i.e., older or more skilled thieves train their younger or less skilled companions. This view of the tutelage process must be qualified a bit to meet today's conditions as it implied an uncomplicated or almost automatic recruitment process. Today, a good deal of effort might have to be put in by the prospective criminal if he wants to be accepted as an apprentice. The aspiring thief might act like this:

"How did you learn to be a safe-cracker?"
"Well, the theoretical part I picked up in jail. Ya listen to the older guys until your ears are ready to pop off. Then you become buddies, latch on to some clever guy - you picked out someone you

thought was the best. And when ya got out, maybe
ya waited for him - I remember I did. I worked on
the docks and lived at home with my mother, lay
low for a while... In any case, we had a plan...
and then ya gotta go out and do the job under his
supervision. (laughter) That's how you got
training."

The sociologist Prus and the card hustler Sharper
have together analyzed the hustler's way of living.
They point out that the established hustlers are
usually not open or friendly towards newcomers. The
latter have to prove themselves. I think this is
quite general in the criminal world. The inhabitants
cannot afford someone who draws attention to the
group, someone who talks too much, etc. Even in the
tightly-knit group of card hustlers, who need to
spread their knowledge, there is always a certain
amount of competition, of testing and the worry that
someone may disappear from the group taking his
aquired knowledge with him. This makes the tutelage
process one of "learn as you go", instead of an open
diffusion of knowledge. Below, a card hustler on how
he "learnt the ropes":

You see them hemming and hawing and stalling
around. You wonder what they are doing, so you
watch and see what's going on. Now, once you find
out on your own, then they open up to you. But
it's not like they're going to say "Well, this is
what we're going to do..." They don't do that -
it's basically learn as you go. And, the more you
learn, the more your status goes up. (1977:58)

Furthermore, the tutelage process is sometimes
rejected since not instructing others can be
functional: the others cannot rat on you. A comment
from a study of thieves and problems of selling
stolen goods:
Information as to the origin and destination of
goods is cut off so that the distribution of
knowledge is minimized even among colleagues. (West,

1974:247)

McIntosh (1971) has remarked that most crimes described in autobiographies of criminals are similar (even if they seem unique) in that there is a pattern reflecting different cultures and periods. Naturally, one does learn from one another and all are collectively restricted by the external environment. However the existence of creativity **per se** must not be denied. Many of my respondents were full of pride when they told me of different ways they had managed to earn money: they were proud because **they** saw their activities as original. A comment by Martin in the biography *My Life in Crime*, is illustrative:

> Lots of things I've sat down and figured out myself, they may not have been original, probably somebody been doing them since the beginning of time, but nobody ever told me about them ... (1952:189)

Criminals are perhaps a bit in the same boat as the Russian living completely isolated in the country, who supposedly invented the bicycle fifty years after it was out on the market.

Summing up, there is a high demand for creativity and inventiveness if one is to make it in the criminal world, due to the above-described difficulties in establishing contacts, the non-automatic process of tutelage, lack of possibilities for "rehearsing", etc. These specific problems are one reason that criminals have a certain pride in "making it".

Pride in getting by

As has been stated above, there often seems to be more **individual** planning and effort behind crime than in many other types of occupations. This way of figuring out angles to succeed in different ventures also seems to be a challenge and a source of pride.

Being proud of creativity in illegal money-making

activities is not reserved to the successful thieves. Shover writes about how addicts react to the stigma attached to them by the good thieves, who complain that they cannot steal in an organized way but take advantage of their own neighborhood, family, etc. The addicts admit that they are not successful as thieves, but demand recognition for their skills. One of his interviewed addicts thus states:

> I think, in order for a man to live out there in the streets by his own wits, and his own ability, and his own initiative ... takes more than a notion, you know. It's not easy, it's a pretty hard road, you know... I would say as far as ingenuity and in the things he thinks of and ideas and what not, I wouldn't say he's inferior to any other thief. (1971:51-52)

Making it by using one's own ingenuity is not only a source of pride but is also "fun". The jazz musician and former addict David Allyn confirms that some of the things one does while almost "down and out" can, at least in retrospect, be viewed with a certain appreciation:

> I was the first one to rent a $1,500 camera, carry it uptown, take off the serial number and sell it for $700. Necessity is the mother of invention. When you become an addict, all the energies go into manipulating and cunning. It's so sick, it's funny too, but it's so sick. (Los Angeles Times, July 25, 1982:84)

Knowledge as investment

After a certain amount of time engaged in illegal activities, obviously many legal doors close for the criminal. One becomes therefore more reliant on the criminal ones in terms of financial as well as social support. Another process which can lead to a higher involvment is more neglected: one's own investment in a criminal world.

Getting to know the ropes of the criminal life is quite time-consuming. The inhabitants in this world have invested a lot in getting to know the necessary people, and in being known as a trustworthy person, etc. The time spent in prison can be seen in the same light: from the point of view of investment, it can serve to enforce commitment to crime. First of all, it would be wasteful not to use the skills one picked up while in prison, and secondly, the time spent there is a positive merit only in the world of crime.

This investment can of course lead to a feeling that this life owes you something. The card and dice hustlers that Prus and Sharper (1977) studied thus expressed a feeling that "hustling owed them something": a debt that could only be realized through greater participation. Maybe this is part of the reason for the dream of the big score. This was usually not mentioned, in other ways than with a laugh, but the existence of the dream (even if most are quite realistic in thinking they will not make it) might be due to a feeling of "Just that one, because this life owes me something."

3
BEATING THE SYSTEM

To lead a criminal life requires cunning and inventiveness not only in conjunction with crime, but also in general to beat the system.[1] These strategies can be said to be ways of actively defending a criminal lifestyle by outwitting the system through rational means and a way of showing that one can exercise control.

Beating the system is something not only so-called professional thieves are engaged in.[2] Young thieves, the less skilled, etc. in my study also used these techniques when they could while committed to criminal life.

Having a front for the authorities

One of the main strategies, of course, is having a front (Goffman, 1959). This can include techniques of using the welfare office for reasons other than the conventional one of getting money. As a young drug dealer described it, the reason for his being on welfare was not the need for cash but to have a front to pacify other official agencies which might otherwise wonder how he made his living. This young dealer was also quite proud of having been able to supply a girlfriend and two other friends during this time with drugs, food, lodging, etc., while at the same time being able to establish himself in a nice apartment with expensive furniture. Plate (1975) recounts similar methods of using the welfare office by American criminals.

The need to keep a front vis-a-vis the police is obviously important. The account below of what it takes is probably exaggerated but it reveals an "ideal" view how this is done:

> "If you make a good haul (break-in), you can buy yourself a better car, so it'll take more time for the police to catch up with you. You sort of take care of your background, protect your rear. Because if you protect your rear the police won't find you as easy as otherwise. But it can get expensive."
>
> "How?"
>
> "Well,it's like ... If you're gonna make it you have to wear a mask for the outside world. You'll have to have two apartments, they'll cost you some rent. You have to, you **should** have a broad that you live with ... she'll cost money ..."

Using one's criminal identity

Prisoner organizations can be easy preys for criminals committed to their lifestyle. Discussing opportunists in organizations set up to help prisoners, the American sociologist Irwin describes them in the following way:

> Many opportunists, however, found the movement especially suited to their talents and needs. It offered them access to "movement chicks", fame, some financial support, a front for illegal activities, and a defense - that of police harassment because of their political activities - when they were arrested. (1980:120)

Later he describes the infiltration of one such criminal into the Prisoners' Union, which he used as a front for illegal activities:

Because of his reputation as a bully and informer
in prison, he was disliked by most of the ex-
prisoners present, but his aggressive display in
the style of the "hog" (a tough convict) won him
election of the first board of directors ... he
participated in the planning and public activities
of the union, always presenting himself as a true
convict who was looking out for the interest of
the prisoners .. All the while, he continued a
full "street life": pimping, hustling, and dealing
drugs. (Ibid.:121)

According to my respondents, this unintended usage
of prisoners' organizations is not exclusive for the
US. One thief in my study who like to have a sort of
mafia organization because it would mean protection,
said for example:

Like you as students take care of each other and
accept each other and have clubs, unions. We don't
have any fraternities, well, we've got some
disguised ones, RFHL and we've got KRUM where
thieves meet but ... You should just know how many
business deals that are made there behind the
scenes.

RFHL and KRUM, which are reportedly used in this
unintended way, are organizations that are supposed
to rehabilitate and help prisoners and addicts on a
voluntary basis.
One can also use one's criminal past. This is an
advantage if one intends, for example, to stay
unemployed. An old thief told me about a period when
he had been out of work. I interrupted and asked,
"Why, couldn't you get a job?" His reply is
instructive for those of us who believe that for
criminals, having a job is enough to "readjust"
them.

Sure I could but I didn't want one. I got a lot of
referrals from the employment office and you have

to go there during probation so I went over to the
employer and when they asked why I hadn't had a
job for a while I told them I had been in the pen
for the last years and when they asked why, I told
them, well, at my last job I stole from my fellow
workers, and then I didn't get the job ... (with a
straight face). It was a good thing since I didn't
want to work (laughter) ...

Needless to say, this man never stole from his
fellow workers and when he wanted to go straight, he
used quite different strategies to achieve that
goal. According to another former thief this method
– pretending to have stolen from fellow workers –
was quite common and used as a last resource to
harden even the softest of tolerant potential
employers.

Manipulating rehabilitation measures

The last quote can be said to exemplify the
difference between constituent and strategic norms,
which can be described as having a moral versus a
technical connotation.[3] The situation that occurs
when both of these are used is a "game within the
game". In this context, criminals can thus be seen
as following the constituent norms overtly but
adhering privately to their strategic norms. Aubert
(1979) notes that referring to norms can be means in
a strategy and can be used contrary to the original
goals of the norms. For prisoners, the general goal
of rehabilitation and the norms that say one should
encourage this can, of course, be used in ways that
were not anticipated.
   A former thief:

Some years ago you could get your drivers' licence
inside the pen and at that time many nagged about
it until they got permission to take it because
they claimed becoming a driver was the only way
they could make it when they got out. Bud they
only wanted it so they could drive legally while

out scoring at nights.

Another example is the use of job-related rehabilitation. A man whom I labelled a "prisoner politician", who worked for prisoners' rights and better conditions (he was respected by the other inmates as far as I could judge but must have had a hard job at times), discussed such a program with two others, a young man clearly committed to his lifestyle and an older thief who stated from the beginning that he had never wanted to work and that was why he supported himself by crime.

> The young man: "But when I get out, they're never gonna get me to work, never ... I'm never gonna put myself in a workshop to turn or weld or something."
> The politician: "But they'll fix an apartment, work. Damn it, they'll arrange everything for you."
> The young man: "Yeah, sure, but it's a matter of **wanting** to work when you get out. I don't want to. But during imprisonment I guess I could accept their ..."
> The older man: "You mean use it to get a good daypass or something?"
> The young man: "Yeah."
> The older man: "Well, it's not a waste of time ..."
> The young man: "Yeah, I guess so, you'll have that education later, even if you don't want it now."
> The politician: "Well, to me it's wrong to start something that you don't take up later."
> The older man: "Well, I don't know many who do."
> The politician: "The percentage is high, eight out of thirty-five, that's pretty good anyhow."
> The young man: "I've got a lot of friends who've done that stuff, and received daypasses and then when they've been released, it's just like 'Why the hell should we go to work in a factory?'"

For those who either cannot get a job or do not want

one, a phony job is a way to get parole. Even though
the practice of false certificates might not be too
common, a couple of inmates referred to it. Anyhow,
here is a discussion between an inmate who did not
want to work but got a phony job the last time he
had been out of prison and a young inmate not having
the necessary connections to get one:

> The first inmate: "You can get yourself a
> certificate saying that you're employed by a small
> business somewhere. They'll check if the firm is
> registered and of course it is, and that's it.
> It's a way to get out."
> The young inmate: "I don't know how to get
> something like that. I don't have the connections,
> haven't been around those kind of people ..."
> The first inmate: "You've got to have contacts,
> you've got to know where to go. If you don't have
> the knowledge you won't get anything ... Last time
> I was out on a thing like that I had such
> unbelievable luck that when the probation officer
> came to check, I just happened to be there on
> other business."
> The interviewer: "Couldn't you get a real job
> there?"
> The first inmate: "Yeah, sure I could, but I
> didn't want it."

After stating this he added that he had supported
himself by crime since 1960 except for six years,
and there was no reason why he should take a lower-
paid job.

This technique seems to work in the United States
as well. According to Dunn, the convict in *The Time
Game*, he got out through his father's arranging a
"shuck job" on the outside which he paid some money
for. His comment about the prison officials:
"They're so easy to beat it's pitiful." (Manocchio
and Dunn, 1970:236)

Abstention programs are another example of
society's readjustment efforts that can be
manipulated. They can even be used as a service

instead of as rehabilitation. The sociologist Waldorf in his book *Careers in Dope* has described how:

> More often than not he goes to treatment to avoid some pressure being exerted upon him; seldom is it because he wants to give up drugs. If an abstention program is not aware of addict's motivations and actually tests them, the program comes to be used by the addict in ways that were never intended: as a service, rather than as rehabilitation; as a temporary shelter ; as a place in which to clean up in order to get high again or to manage one's habit more easily. (1973:24)

An addict can sometimes get out of prison or shorten his time there and be admitted instead to a rehabilitation program. Some of those I interviewed stated that they pretended that they wanted to quit drugs only in order to make use of this possibility. Below an example from an American addict:

> "Both times I took Article Nine," P___ said. That's when the bulls have you on a burglary rap, and you sign to go to a hospital to be cured of addiction. Most addicts take Article Nine, and then go right back to drugs when they get out." (Bowers, 1967:54)

It is thus important to take into account the individual's wishes and interests at certain times in his life. Prus and Sharper, writing about card and dice hustlers, emphasize situations, investments and oppurtunity structures as being important for involvement - be it in legal or illegal activities:

> Persons assess recognized options vis-a-vis feasibility in promoting their interests as they define their interest **at that time.** (my emphasis)(1977:167)

This former thief emphasizes for example the importance of **wanting** to go straight:

> In the beginning you'll have to take whatever shitty job you can get and I got pretty good help, requisition for work clothes and ordinary clothes. I even got help to buy a motor bike and money to start off with ... many who get things like that will use or sell requisitions and buy liquor instead. I used to do that myself. That's how it works for those who **don't want** to straighten up.

Some of the ways described above seem to be common knowledge for members in different deviant subcultures but it is up to the individual whether he chooses to "work them" or not; and if so, if he has the skills, contacts, etc. to be able to succeed.

Finally, it is interesting that even if one wants to leave crime, one may have to use one's wits to get out on one's own terms. This young man wants to quit drugs but not change his lifestyle which very much centered around cars. He is currently studying at a technical high school where he is supposed to continue after prison:

> "Are you going to use that?"
> "Well, I don't know. You have to have something to show, see ..."
> "Are you going to continue as before?"
> "No, not as I've lived so far. But I can't drop everything, I just can't. Selling and buying cars is something I want to do but that doesn't sound good enough to the authorities so I have to have something that looks good to them."

Giving a sense of control

Beating the system has in addition to instrumental value also symbolic value, by giving a sense of being in control of a rather unpredictable life.

Zola (1964) studied men engaged in off-track

betting on horses at a bar in a working-class area. Through their knowledge and skill in selecting horses, they gained recognition and attention in the group: winning meant "beating the system". The "system", which they frequently mentioned , referred more to life or fate than a principle underlying the races. Thus, the obvius satisfaction a safe-cracker showed in telling me how he had cheated a social worker is, I believe, not only restricted to the relationship between the two:

He was fresh from school you know and thought he could reform me, but I taught him and after half a year he quit. I don't think he's ever gonna work as a probation officer again ... (laughter).

4
BUSINESS ORIENTATION

In a world of complex organisations, the hustler defines himself as an entrepreneur, and indeed, he is the last of the competitive entrepreneurs ... The political conservative should applaud all that individual initiative. (Horton, 1977:67)

The wish to have a business

One of the things that struck me while interviewing was the common dream of having a small firm: a car repair shop, a small farm, etc.

In the questionnaire given to 101 inmates in a study in 1978, the inmates were asked what they would like to do or be (table 6). The different alternatives given were based on types of jobs that were mentioned in taped interviews or seen as possible alternatives for this group (such as gardening or farming, cook or factory worker). Almost everyone of those who answered wanted to have a small firm of his own, while only four percent wanted to be a factory worker.

In the later questionnaire, administered in 1981, the inmates and the control group were asked if they would like to own a business or a small firm (table 7).

Table 6.   "Would you like to do or to be as the
            following very much, much, little, or
            very little?"

%	Very much or much	Very little or little
Have your own small firm (car repair shop, etc.)	95	5
Work with children or young people	74	26
Photographer	71	29
Electrician	63	37
Work with "socially misadjusted"	62	38
Car salesman	58	42
Car mechanic	58	42
Work with the sick	56	44
Sailor	48	52
Taxi driver	45	55
Gardening or farm work	45	55
Cook	43	57
Lumberjack	32	68
Carpenter	32	68
Waiter	21	79
Plumber	20	80
Crane operator	17	83
Welder	10	90
Factory worker	4	96

Note: Around a third did not answer or answered that
they did not know.

Table 7.   "Would you like to own a business or
            a small firm?"

%	Inmates	Control group Blue-collar	White-collar
Yes	64	50	40
No	18	19	31
Don't know	18	31	29
Sum	100	100	100
N	(137)	(104)	(92)

This time those interested in owning a business were fewer than in the first result from 1978. The difference in approach probably accounts for the difference in reply: the 1981 questionnaire asks how many actually want to have a business, the 1978 one, what they prefer in comparison to other legal types of work.

The thieves indicate a remarkably high wish to own a business. The desire of the addicts is, as expected, a bit lower, as shown in the next question where a comparison is made from SIFO sample.

Table 8. "I would not mind starting a business of my own."

%	Agree	Disagree	No opinion	Sum	N
Traditional thieves	76	8	16	100	(37)
Addicts	53	24	24	100	(17)
All inmates	67	13	20	100	(115)
SIFO	48	34	17	100	(125)

All inmate groups seem however to enjoy **doing** business, to a higher degree than the SIFO sample:

Table 9. "I enjoy buying and selling things (doing business)."

%	Agree	Disagree	No opinion	Sum	N
Inmates	61	22	17	100	(116)
SIFO	32	45	23	100	(125)

It can be added that the dream among Swedish thieves of having a business seems to be shared by their American brothers. A quote from Shover on the "good burglar" (i.e., so defined by other burglars):

His great ambition is to invest his money as to have a steady, secure and legitimate source of income. In his mind he typically sees this, and freedom from supervision of others ("be my own boss") epitomized in the small businessman. (1971:131-132)

Having had a business

Many of the interviewees dreamed of having a small firm in the future, while quite a few also stated that they had actually had one.

Table 10.   "Have you ever had a business or a small firm of your own?"

%	Inmates	Control group
Yes	26	5
Yes, a criminal one	5	-
No	69	95
Sum	100	100
N	(143)	(198)

A third of the inmates stated that they had had a business - legal or illegal.[1] Compared to the control group, this is quite a high number: of those, only 5% stated that they had had a business or a small firm of their own.[2] It can also be mentioned here that 14% of the inmates' fathers - compared to 5% of the control groups' - had had a business of their own.

The businesses that the interviewees had owned varied from the inmate who in a taped interview stated that he had 13 people working for him in a construction firm to that of the used car dealer with his business in his pocket, and others, who had grown vegetables, potatoes, etc. Most of them, however, had had a one-man type of firm.

Compared to the SIFO sample, more of the interviewed inmates also considered themselves good in bargaining - a business-related skill (table 11). In this context it is interesting to note that many of the inmates actually were contemptuous towards those who engaged in bargaining for "petty things", which their orientation towards money and

Table 11.   "I am good in bargaining."

%	Agree	Disagree	No opinion	Sum	N
Inmates	35	39	26	100	(115)
SIFO	21	52	27	100	(125)

consumption as men-of-the-world would not permit them to do. I have, however, seen some of them engaged in bargaining for their own amusement, in situations where this could be done without disrupting the image of themselves as men who handle money in a careless way. There is however probably a difference here between those who sell to "civilians" or buy stolen goods themselves - in these areas there are possibilities for bargaining. The thief who sold to an established fence, on the other hand, often had to accept a given offer.

The criminal world as an economic world

We have seen that the role of entrepreneur is attractive. Hence, the question arises whether the inmates view their criminal activities in terms of business. If so, how can crime (stealing, drug dealing, etc.) be compared with the legal business world? In the analysis below, which is by no means complete, I have concentrated on issues covered by my material, such as investment, contacts, etc. I will also discuss matters which might not directly belong to a market analysis, but nonetheless are important in this context, for example, the reputation of the actor.

One of the classical scholars in sociology, Veblen, saw the similarities between businessmen and criminals in this way:

The ideal pecuniary man is like the ideal delinquent in his unscrupulous conversion of goods and persons to his own ends, and in a callous disregard of feelings and wishes of others and of the remote effects of his actions, but he is unlike him in possessing a keener sense of status and in

working more farsightedly to a remoter end.
(1912:237)

Status, however, is important for thieves and also
drug dealers, but this will be discussed later. For
the moment, we can add that not only Veblen, but
also some criminologists have compared thieves with
businessmen. Inciardi, for example, has described
the professional thief's attitude towards stealing
in the following way:

To the trained professional thief, **stealing is a
business** ... Like other commercial enterprises,
theft involves hard work of planning and execution.
Business possibilities, conditions, returns,
locations, opportunities, new methods - all the
factors affecting economic feasibility of theft are
approached in the same manner as other business
pursuits. (1974:333)

The criminal world as a world of free competition

A former thief, who was proud of having been a good
thief but wanted to quit because "all that counts
here is money, money and prestige", made the
following comment:

Everyone there can have a high income as well as a
good reputation in a criminal way ... But like the
society outside, it's not many who can make it ...
It takes quite a lot of ruthlessness and lack of
feeling for others: to put it plainly, cruelty. In
the criminal world there are no values at all, so
the most ruthless will be best off.

"Ruthlessness", however, seems to be appreciated by
some. Many talked, with a certain enjoyment, about
times when they managed to cheat someone in a deal,
a typical **caveat emptor** attitude. The common
attitude seems to be: you get cheated but then cheat
others in turn, "business is business":

I sold some black and white TV sets thinking they
were color TV's. I didn't know at that time that I

had gotten cheated myself. They were all together somewhere, and I didn't look at them. Well, this guy who bought them from me in his turn sold them as color TV's. He's never admitted he made a lousy deal or accused me. There are many funny things like that, that's happened, you know ...

Working one's way up

If one sees the criminal world as a business where free competition rules, the possibility of working oneself up by using one's brains or 'elbow grease' in the old-fashioned entrepreneurist way ought to exist. This seems to be, or at least is claimed to be, the case. Some of the inmates state in the interviews that they have done so, either by different business deals or by gaining respect in the criminal world and thereby working oneself up the ladder.

When I get out of the pen, I usually use my start-off money[3] to buy a car - that's number one, the most important thing. After that, I'll fix some stuff to sell on credit , and I get it so cheap that I can make a profit and use it to buy larger amounts to sell. So I've always started off that way ...

If one does not have the contacts that allow one to sell on credit, one can start with stealing instead. This is a good way, according to some interviewees, because a crowbar is cheap - you can even steal that too, if necessary. After collecting a small capital in this way, some reported that they invested it in the more lucrative business of drugs. According to Plate (1975), this first capital is called "seed money" among American criminals.

Investments

Investments can be viewed in terms of either time or money. Crime as business is obviously time-consuming in many ways, but this will not be discussed further here. Monetary investments, however, do not seem to be a vital issue for the majority of thieves – those who do not plan and execute big "jobs" such as bank robberies. For the drug dealers, on the other hand, it is important to have capital.

"You need money?"
"Yeah, quite a lot today."
"How do you get that?"
"Well, as I said, stealing is foreign to me. But you might have a bit in the bank or you might work. So the first time you start out with a thousand crowns and after a while you want more, have higher demands. So you'll have to make a profit on that so you'll have some capital to make further investments with. And right now the profit is so high that you'll always get your money back."
"Do you put in money together with some friends?"
"If you just want to smoke, but not if you're selling. Then you buy speculatively."

There is, however, an inter-relationship between stealing and drugs in the way that some made their capital through stealing and then invested it in drugs – a way to get started. As was shown above, some do not want to steal. Most of the interviewed inmates, however, did not object to this practice. An addict in a rehabilitation program:

Some begin with stealing to get some money. Then they buy themselves a small amount of drugs and set themselves up in business.

The use of drugs can automatically bring one into business and thus solve the economical problems, at least for the moment. A former addict even claimed he had more money while he was an addict than otherwise:

During that time I never had any problems, was

never short of money.

In comparison then with a legal business, a criminal business seems to be easier to start, since less investment is needed. This fact might even be one of the attractions that draws one to illegal business.

Contacts with buyers, fences, etc.

Personal contacts that depend on trust are of course essential in the criminal world.

Sellerberg (1982) has argued that the opposite is true for transactions in the modern society. Due to different regulations protecting the consumer, he or she no longer needs to have a personal knowledge of the salesman. In the criminal world, on the other hand, the sellers must create this confidence in their customers, except, of course, when the demand is so high that the seller can call the shots, as for example when drugs are hard to get hold of.

The actual making of contacts can be difficult. As has been discussed earlier, finding a fence for example is not as easy as one might assume. One respondent had even made a business of "knowing people". He sold names of buyers of stolen goods. Doing this, he charged both the thief and the fence and thereby had a quite lucrative information 'bureau' of his own.

Contacts for drug buying or selling are as important and not easily acquired. An Iranian I talked to for example had run into great difficulties when he tried to sell the heroin he had smuggled in and planned to live on in Sweden because he did not know the people in the game. The prices for drugs also vary of course depending on how much one moves in the right circles:

If you're in business and at the top, you'll have contacts, but if not, you'll have to go down to the park yourself and buy a small bag for a lot of money.

Thus, contacts are important both for supporting your own addiction at a lesser cost and also for being in business: being able to buy for selling. Some of the respondents even said that contacts "meant everything" in criminal life - without them, one was lost.

The next issue that confront the thief is **whom** to sell to. Not selling to professional fences is looked down upon by the "good burglars", not only as being beneath them, but also practically - they have to have someone who can handle large amounts. They sometimes had to unload, for example, a whole truckful of cigarettes, or other big scores. They thought furthermore that those who did sell directly to the buyer did not know in advance where to dump their goods. Especially for younger thieves, this was sometimes the case, but some of those who sold directly were actually quite rational in arguing for not selling to fences. The fence is obviously a middleman, and can thus not afford to pay a price as high as someone who is going to use the goods himself. Thus the price was an argument for selling directly.

Another reason for direct sales was that it was more secure selling to many, since that made an arrest for major theft less likely. Here, the police would find only small quantities of the actual amount, that is, if the buyers did not know each other. Furthermore, this type of selling was not always done in a random way. Some thieves had established networks of contacts and thus had prepared channels for delivery: this can be as professional as the practice of selling to a fence, as the "good burglars" did:

You know, if you're in a clothing shop, you know what sizes you can place, so you know what you're looking for. Ann Andersson's a 38 so you'll grab five for her and five in size 52 for her husband, and so on. You plan it because you have to. The sort of fast jobs like running into a store, grabbing a tape-recorder and running out again -

that won't last long, you'll get busted. That's the type of thing you did when you were young, you know.

Similarly, the American criminologist Inciardi (1974) writes about stealing to order. A number of his informants also stole items in a predetermined price class and had buyers' "shopping list". According to them, this system was more profitable, and thus preferable to selling to a fence.

Reputation

Once the contacts are made, it is essential for the thief to acquire a reputation for being "good" in different ways, for example being reliable.

Acquiring a reputation for being trustworthy is not only important for social reasons but also for success in business. Selling drugs on credit is common among drug addicts. Often, however, this is not carried out properly. The seller might use too much himself and be unable to pay the bigger dealer. Since neither police nor other legal agencies exists in the criminal world whose function is to collect the missing money, the only resort is violence – using it yourself, or having someone do it for you. But, as a drug dealer said, "It's not much use beating up a guy – you won't get your money back anyway." One older addict was quite proud of his record of never having delayed with his payments. Due to this he had been able to climb in the drug-dealing hierarchy:

"How did you get established as a dealer?"
"That's a tough question. I didn't establish myself, it's just that I've never cheated anyone, which is really uncommon in the dealing trade, where bad shit is sold and where people are charged too much and all that stuff. I've never done that, always fixed my debts immediately and seldom bought on credit. I'd done some small scale dealing ... your reputation spreads around quickly

if you've blown someone or made a bad deal or
something. It's only one percent who haven't and
that's the percentage that'll get the chance ...
so that's the way I've got it. If you get a hecto
or half a kilo on credit without paying in
advance, you've established yourself as honest."

One can also try to establish and make use of a good
reputation by selling cheap. A man, not dealing in
drugs but working as a fence, talked about getting a
reputation by using "good prices" in order to make
steady customers. When we discussed selling to
ordinary people, which he had done, he stated:

You should be aware that everything is possible to
fix, even though it might take some time. By this,
I don't mean that you have to go stealing it
yourself ... and if you don't earn a lot on this
particular deal there might be more occasions, you
see ...

Finally, the importance of a good reputation if you
are to succeed in the criminal world is illustrated
by the thief who told me he quit drugs because his
reputation had deteriorated, which he could not
afford.

Consumer demands

Like other businessmen, criminals need to know what
is sellable for the moment. Lewis, who has
emphasized the rationality of hustling, writes about
the consumer demand dimension in this context, and
claims that the hustler engages in:

... a market analysis of considerable
sophistication. He has to take on goods which are
likely to have a fast turnover on the market to
which he has access. This means that the hustler
has to assess accurately local taste and consumer
demand ... Beyond maintaining a market or consumer
analysis, the hustler who is "fencing" must also

work out acceptable profit margins in his
"retailing" operation .. It would indeed be
difficult to find in a legitimate economic
enterprise endeavors which exceed this hustle in
the exercise of sophistication and rationality.
(1970:179-180)

As seen in the quote above, the hustler must be
aware of certain consumer demands in order to make
it. This elderly thief is a good example of what was
stated above:

"What do you steal?"
"That depends on what's sellable for the moment."
"How do you mean?"
"The demand ... the stuff I know works. Everything
from gold, that's always in circulation, to stamp
collections, old coins, drugs ..."

Others have talked about gold as the item that
"sells best these days", tape recorders as
absolutely "out", etc.

Addicts, thieves and business

The heroin user is, in a way, like the compulsive
hard working business executive whose ostensible
goal is the acquisition of money, but whose real
satisfaction is in meeting the inordinate
challenge he creates for himself. (Preble and
Casey, 1969:21)

The authors, who have studied heroin users in New
York, criticize the usual escape theories of
addiction - escaping from life, from psychological
problems or social responsibility, as well as
Cloward and Ohlin's (1960) "double failure" thesis.
This stated that those who neither succeed in the
lawful or the criminal world formed a retreatist
subculture which centered around the consumption of
drugs. Instead, Preble and Casey claim that addicts
are engaged in "aggressively pursuing a career that

is exciting, challenging, adventurous, and rewarding. They are always on the move and must be alert, flexible and resourceful." (Ibid.:22)

The authors even note the heroin user's way of walking. It is purposeful and fast as if he is late for an important meeting - which he usually is. A Swedish former addict pointed out the same thing for me. The way to recognize the "real" addicts in the streets was the way they walked, and he described this in the same manner as the authors above.

The addicts in Preble and Casey's study are thus occupied with "taking care of business", and this is reflected in the answer to questions like "How are you doing?", or "What's happening?": "Taking care of biz." The quest for heroin, then, for them is a quest for a meaningful life : through the gratification of the challenges and excitement it provides in their life, more than through the biological gratification according to the authors.

Sutter, who has used an approach similar to the authors' above when studying addicts, emphasizes the importance of not putting addicts in one category but differentiating them into several groups with different lifestyles. These groups are based both on a career formation and on different beliefs and interests. "Players", for example, shift their drug use to hustling:

A player shifts his game from play to "serious business" and a preoccupation with a master crime scheme for the future. Hustling appears to many as the road to an elite type of existence, success, prestige, and luxury. (1969:816)

Sutter also notes that the player performs a crucial role in the adolescent marketplace, and mediates the flow of drugs and hot merchandise from adult hustlers to adolescent consumers. Drug use takes an instrumental slant and the theme of enterprise supplants the theme of sociability.

Thieves, on the contrary, seem to have an inverted relation to drugs and money. After becoming interested in the profit available, they have to use drugs in order to know what they are selling. Some reported that they got addicted in this way.

Thieves are also involved in business activities in a somewhat different way than addicts. Those who steal goods instead of money have to have a fair idea of what they are stealing, as mentioned above in Chapter 2. If this is jewelry or art, they have to have more than a common knowledge about these items. A fence, claiming that he does not cheat the burglars, says smilingly, however:

> Most of these young thieves, they can't recognize stones or they'll think white gold is silver, and can't understand that there are diamonds attached to a ring like that. So after I examine what they bring, I'll ask them "What do you want?", and they'll give a price ...

Not only fences are in a position to take advantage of their knowledge: thieves can do the same provided that they do not sell to those in the know:

> "Once I even sold a Concert Hall (a stereo) that costs seven hundred crowns to him for fifteen hundred."
> "Didn't he get angry?"
> "No, he never noticed."

The older thieves seemed to have fixed prices with fences and did not engage in bargaining as much as the younger ones. A thief who sells to professional fences:

> "Do you get what you ask for your goods?"
> "There are fixed prices and more or less accepted rules, like how much you get for your gold at the moment."

Another consideration is not to sell too cheaply, as addicts are said to do. They "dump the market":

> There have been times when things have been hard to sell ... but gold is the same as money, it's

always possible to sell but it's a question of
getting the right price for it. You can sell
everything, you know, but the question is how much
you want. You don't want to give things away so
you'll have to try to get something that's
proportionate to its value ... And then you have
those damned heroinists that dump the market -
they'll sell at whatever price they can get, as
long as they get their fix.

Yet another rule for thieves is never to do business
with addicts, as they "snitch".

They aren't trustworthy and can't keep their cool.
If you do - if there aren't ten running after you
the next day, then you can easily count on being
busted.

Types of business orientation

Action oriented

Owning a business means different things for
different people. Criminals want to consider
themselves "businessmen" rather than actually having
a business somewhere. This distinction can be made
by saying that the first is more oriented to fast
deals and action. In a comparison of fast food
franchisees and cleaning franchisees, Sklar
described the first group as action-seekers:
Contrary to the notion that small businessmen are
committed to a lifetime of building up a specific
business ... Any particular business is treated as a
gambling event ... His commitment is not to
ownership of a small business but to "small business
ownership". (1977:44)
The difference between the groups was reflected in
their respective language. Goffman (1967) has
pointed out that an action-seeking lifestyle
includes expressions such as "blowing it", "having
it made", and "having something going for oneself".
This terminology was used by the fast food

franchisees. The interviewed criminals often described their illegitimate activities in a similar fashion. One example of this:

> You can **work yourself up** by starting out with a small capital and **invest** it in drugs and thereby **get something going for yourself** if you are **smart**. When you are **in business**, if you're a drug dealer, you've gotta **administer** the business, which you can do sitting at a restaurant giving orders to your subordinates. When you have **blown it**, you have to start all over again. (My emphasis)

No organized crime syndicates for thieves

The ideal in this world of business among most of those interviewed is not, however, to break into big business in crime like the mafia or so-called organized crime. They are thus not striving for rationality in the sense of an effective division of labor, something that Cressey (1972) sees as characterizing organized crime. The emphasis is instead on being a small independent businessman and having control of oneself and one's criminal projects. Many stated that "... in this world everybody works for himself." The following quote by an elderly burglar can be seen as quite typical:

> "Thefts aren't organized - all of these people are their own businessmen."
> "Do they want it that way?"
> "Yeah, I believe so ... and that's what gives the best profit as well."

According to a question about how crime was organized in Sweden, few believed that there was anything resembling a mafia there and few stated that they would like to have a more organized crime scene. One of the really committed criminals, who incidentally did not believe that the mafia existed in Sweden, emphasized the lack of independence this would imply:

"Do you think that criminality ought to be organized?"
"No, it's the freedom I'm looking for, I want to have a free life. I don't want to be dependent on anything. Organized crime, what in hell is it? Some kind of a mafia? No, I don't believe in that." (with contempt)
"You don't think it exists in Sweden?"
"There might be people who think that they belong to such stuff. They've read too many thrillers."
"Is it foreign groups?"
"I don't know, but you have seen how it's been lately, they shoot each other and I don't know what that's supposed to be good for." (laughter)
"I don't believe it exists in the States either, it's ridiculous."

This man viewed some of the foreigners as trying to act as if they were involved in organized crime and using violence as a means to an end in their business dealings. The following quote indicates how he resents their greediness and profit-hunger and how he values his freedom:

"I've gotten to know many of the foreigners that have clubs and have been involved in some of their businesses. There is so much unfriendliness in these foreign gangs ... their attitudes are different, they're trying to **get** something all the time and that's what their activities are all about. So you feel as if you're used .. Many of them are really greedy and as soon as you're doing business with them they want some sort of security to keep you in line with, like a family or something ..."
"That's quite a threat."
"Yeah, but I don't have one. I'm free in their eyes, I've always been free both inside the pen and outside because if things don't suit me, I'll tell anyone. And if this doesn't suit anyone, I'll just skip 'em and it doesn't matter how much or

how attractive it (a business or a deal) is."

An American thief confirms the same attitude of preferring to be a lone wolf rather than losing his independent status to an organization:

> A thief is an outlaw. In more ways than one ... If you're in the rackets you're in an organization. You can go up but you go up slow. If you're a burglar or a stickup man or any type of specific thief, you're strictly operating as an individual, you're an independent worker, you have a different feeling about things, you're not tied down . (Martin, 1952:139)

In addition to wanting to remain free from organizations, thieves might also reject the long-term monetary goals that they see in the organized groups, goals which clash with the aversion to planning in general and the preference for spur-of-the-moment spending. In their view those criminals connected with organized crime have adjusted to conventional norms of planning and investing and thereby have missed the real meaning of the criminals lifestyle. King, in his biography, explains why the rackets did not appeal to him:

> A thief cannot go into that, a buck don't mean nothing to him. It's real hard for a thief to plan, what you call, by the month. If I got a buck in my pocket, then I spend the buck. If I ain't got it, then I look around for one. You're trained that way for years so to become adjusted to work for the rackets is very hard for you ... A thief cannot become a succesful businessman. On the average he can't. He hasn't got a chance. He has got to stay in his own business. That's why the syndicates are still staying in the rackets. They spend money getting into these legitimate businesses they hardly don't make no money in it. (Chambliss and King, 1972:68)

Even without the consideration of organized criminality, one might still refrain from expanding one's business, keeping a low level of activity in order for it to remain fun:

> First you do it (deal hasch) to make some bread. Then you think it's fun. Then you start getting too big and it gets to be a hustle. Then you want out so you pack it up. After a while you're dealing small and it becomes fun again. (Goldberg, 1973:86)

Even if the burglary market is not organized on any big scale according to the interviewees, the drug market is. For some, the increasing level of organization of the drug market has meant that the fascination in using drugs is gone. An older former thief and addict claims that this was the reason that he quit using drugs:

> The smuggling grew more sophisticated and that meant more money being involved and that in its turn meant more organization. The "money people" wanted to protect their investments so that there was profit left. It got to be a shittier atmosphere ... and that's the way it's been going.

He went on to talk with nostalgia of the good old days: when it used to be fun going to Germany with friends and buying uppers in drugstores or asking obese women to get prescriptions from unsuspicious doctors for amphetamines.

Possible reasons

Merton's innovators?

In Merton's (1957) famous typology of adjustments to social structure and societal values for individuals, thieves are viewed as "innovators" since they adhere to society's goals of material sucess, but use alternative means to reach the goals. This has been widely discussed among subcultural scholars in criminology. One major critique is the assumption of one general goal - status through material success - in society.

It has been said that in Europe with its class tradition, there are different goals and values in different social strata. Merton however limited his discussion to America, with its ideology that everybody has a chance of reaching the top: "the American dream". Bell has thus argued in the article *Crime as an American Way of Life* that criminality was used by immigrant groups to achieve a certain standard until they reached a position in society where this no longer was necessary.

An American sociologist, Lewis (1970), describes black slum hustlers' business orientation as a reflection of common goals and values similar to the rest of society. They accept both rationality and achievement. The author even argues that the more conventionally socialized, the greater probability of deviance if born in a slum. This is, however, as I see it, dependent on what one means by socialization. I would guess that the hustlers' families do not want them to be pimps, numbers runners, or bootleggers, even if it brings them material success, and even if these activities, if successful, might bring them the reputation of being smart among the younger people in the slum environment.

Merton's view implies a homogenous culture for America which, as Miller (1958) has argued, is not even necessarily true: Miller emphasized the importance specifically of the lower class culture in generating gang delinquency. If one follows Miller one must conceive that not all criminals are motivated by a striving towards what Merton sees as common goals. West's (1974) "serious thieves" - a sample of American non-professional thieves - are for example not described as wanting big material success, but are content to have enough money to get by on without having to resort to what they see as a dull 9-5 job. This was also the main reason stated by my respondents both to why they engaged in crime and why they wanted a business - their goals were not (as the mafia studied by Cressey (1977)) to join the upper or middle class through illegal means.

Self-independence

One motive for having a business more common than material success was epitomized in statements such as "I want to be my own boss".

Since the respondents generally placed a high value on independence, and often claimed that this was a reason for their criminality, it makes sense that they would try to be independent by being self-employed. Although my knowledge of ex-thieves is limited, my impression (through talking with thieves, some former thieves, correctional personnel, etc.) is that many do start a business when they quit crime. This might well be interpreted as a way of consistently maintaining one's self-image as an independent man.

Having a business of one's own, whether legal or illegal, means not being subordinated to anyone, a wish, or perhaps a need, shared by many different criminal groups. This might even explain the attractions of a variety of criminal lifestyles. Pimps for example are said to rely on themselves rather than work for anyone else: "Independence and manhood are why a player, if he goes on the higher game, will only go into business for himself." (Milners, 1972:260)

The thieves I interviewed, said exactly the same thing. When they talked about the possibility of getting a job as factory worker, they often said, "Well, you value yourself more than that." Thus, in the same manner as the pimps saw the "chump job" as personally degrading, the respondents tended to view an ordinary factory job as something that implied lack of dignity.

Rationality

Regarding crime as business can also imply a consciously calculated rationality. One reason for starting a business - legal or illegal - might be that it is more difficult for them to find employment since most of them do not have work records to cover the time' spent in crime or in prison. A previous card-hustler comments on disinvolvement in hustling in this manner:

> But say a guy wants to go straight ... how is he going to get this legitimate job? Who is going to hire him? What training does he have? ... To get out, you have to have the money to invest in a business of some sort or a friend or a relative who will cut you in on some action. (Prus and Sharper, 1977:131)

Most criminals do not have this amount of money, but some of the interviewees had actually been "cut into some action" by relatives, and in this way tried to go straight. Since 26% of the interviewees stated that they had had a legal business of their own, one can conclude that it is not impossible for them to start one. Some interviewees had even gotten help from social welfare offices to start a firm.

Some ex-criminals may have acquired skills in their previous life of crime that they can use in starting a legal business:

> Stealing in cellars is pretty common among them (addicts) and sometimes they'll sell it to some guy who deals with used stuff. You know x, he's an antique dealer now ... he used this and nowadays he's a legitimate, established antique dealer. He got his apprenticeship stealing in dirty old cellars.

Apart from becoming a legal businessman, crime can in itself be viewed with detachment as business and calculated in rational terms. Some robbers in

Jackson's *In the Life* compared getting caught to a
"bankruptcy" in the business world:

> And crime, we feel, is just like any other
> business. In other words, there's setbacks in
> crime and there's deficits, just like you run a
> business and there's a chance that you might burn
> down or go bankrupt ... Of course, the penalty for
> going bankrupt in crime is much stiffer, but at
> the same time your material gain is much more than
> it is in a regular business. (1972:41-42)

Getting away from the criminal stigma

An important aspect of having a legal business of
your own is that it can protect you from the stigma
of being "an ex-con" in the sense that you can avoid
working closely with people who may look down on
you. An older addict, supporting himself by selling
used cars, says:

> It's something you can do by yourself - decide
> your own working pace, and so on, avoid being a
> slave to the clock, working 9-5. And no one knows
> you. I can't handle working regular nowadays ... I
> guess I could handle the work itself but I can't
> handle being together with ... the people around.

Action

Criminals are often described, here and elsewhere[4],
as action-oriented. It thus makes sense that the
criminal's view of a businessman is one who has an
action-dominated life, a way to an independent and
unregulated existence, as well as a means of having
free time. This interpretation of what it means to
have a business differs a lot from the reality of
the legal businessman, whose life is often highly
organized and quite routinized in order for him to
be successful. In addition, the "straight"
businessman must spend much time on his business and
do a great deal of paper work - something which most

inmates detest.

Doing business, and especially action-oriented business, involves taking chances. Inmates seem to enjoy this more than the average as 46% of the inmates agreed to the statement "I enjoy taking chances", as opposed to only 26% of the SIFO sample agreed. Summing up, criminals can be said to be more interested in the fast, risky deal than the daily running of a family firm. This can lead to an appreciation of the criminal type of business rather than the legitimate.

Legitimate versus criminal business

The respondents saw no difference in honesty between themselves as businessmen and legal businessmen. What then is the difference between them? Some said the latter group are "smarter" or as Eugene, the thief in Martin's biography, said, they are more patient. Talking about a fence who had a legitimate store:

> You can see that the fella that actually handled the merchandise made more than the fella that actually took it. He had the patience to stay in business to handle it, that's all. (1952:119)

Aside from all the problems a legal business would entail and the problems of acquiring it, there might be other attractions in remaining in the illegal world. As mentioned in the preceeding section, there are obviously more thrills and excitement - more action - connected with crime.

A good illustrations of this is one of my respondents who once had a small leather business which he started while he was in prison. When he got out he was offered to continue in cooperation with a saddle-making firm. He did this for a while, but quit when it got to be too much administration and organization. Since he was "too restless" for those types of working conditions, he went back to his former fencing and drug business.

I believe that Goffman's notion of the dilemma for the individual concerning expression versus performance is highly relevant in asking why criminals do not have a legal business:

Those who have the time or talent to perform a task well may not, because of this, have the time or talent to make it apparent that they are performing well. (1959:33)

Most work tasks are poorly designed in terms of allowing the individual an expression of "desired meaning". Therefore, if the individual seeks dramatization of his work-role, a high level of investment must be made to achieve this at the cost of the actual work task. Thus, criminals' wish to **be** businessmen can in this sense not only hinder their concentration on successfully carrying out their legal business goals, but also their illegal ones.[5] A former addict's answer to a question about if he used to go to restaurants can exemplify the feeling that being a businessman is sometimes more appreciated than being successful:

> Well, you go to a restaurant when you're at the top of the hierarchy. If you're in a lot of dealing you'll go to restaurants. All my time there will be used to administer the drug business. Even if you don't have a large amount, the dealing can be quite extensive, lots of transactions, middle hands and stuff ... Usually this is really clumsy but when you're in it you see yourself as really smart and sophisticated.

Others have talked about how criminals in high positions use others to run errands for them, clean their cars, etc. These things seem quite similar to the picture of the old-fashioned hard business leader. All this, being in restaurants, dealing, giving orders, etc., is an express that one, for the moment at least, is a businessman. In Goffman's words, a "dramatic realization":

While in the presence of others, the individual typically infuse his activity with signs which dramatically highlight and portray confirmatory facts that might otherwise remain unapparent or obscure. (1959:30)

There are of course other reasons why criminals do not start a legal business. Apart from the obvious ones, like lack of money, one major problem involves leaving familiar surroundings, old friends, etc. The Milners discuss, for example, the problem of the pimps who attempt to get out: trying to save and build something for the future, etc., while cutting ties simultaneously with all their former associates and the security of their older social network:

When white middle-class people are presented with this view of the hustler as a dedicated capitalist who is trapped in the hustling underworld, a common reaction is "Why don't these people do something about it?" ... But it is an extremely rare individual who can step outside of his culture, and throw away the survival kit with which that culture has provided him ... The tools and attitudes, the cultural lenses upon which a man has learned to depend, cannot be easily discarded for another set. (1972:137)

Consequently, as Shover (1971) has noted in his study of burglars, one of the problems criminals run into if they are to succeed when starting a small legal business is how to keep their former associates away. If their old cronies continue to be in evidence, the question then of course is whether they cannot be kept away or the new business owner wants them to come for reasons given above. The typical individualistic opinion of a former thief:

"I know someone who had a business but he always had a lot of thieves hangin' around."
"Did he have difficulties in saying 'no' to his old pals?"
"Maybe, or probably he didn't want to be away from them at all. They were sittin' there plannin' new scores. He kept it up for half a year, then that was it, he was finished. You can't take care of a business like that."

5
THIEVES CLAIM RESPONSIBILITY

Explanations of criminality

Criminals have often been described as blaming their behavior on external circumstances. Contrary to this belief, most do claim responsibility for their actions and are prepared to take the consequences for them. They do not point the finger at their social background or see themselves as victims of circumstances. This sense of personal responsibility encompasses not only crimes but also norms for making a living. Norms of manliness and responsible adulthood serve as a background for these attitudes. Criminals' action-oriented lives as well as their "marginal man" status can also explain why they are willing to take the blame themselves.

During my first more qualitative studies of criminals in 1977 and 1978, I was surprised by the respondents' refusal to throw the blame on others. Statements such as "I **chose** this because ...", "I'll never work in a factory, I prefer this type of life", etc. made me want to test the issue in a more quantitative way. I also wanted to compare inmates with a comparative sample of non-criminal respondents. The questions were formulated quite straightforwardly: "Whose fault is it if someone becomes a criminal?" and to the inmates, "Whose

fault is it that you became a criminal?". The
responses given can be seen below.

Table 12.

%	All inmates	Thereof thieves	Thereof addicts	Control group Blue-collar	White-collar
It is my (their) own fault	71	74	50	50	46
Society's fault	30	32	44	46	27
My (their) upbringing	27	33	11	58	71
Drugs	18	11	33	26	17
Alcohol	11	12	0	20	8
Friends		3	6	40	26
N	(137)	(84)	(18)	(103)	(93)

The results confirmed my initial idea that thieves
in particular consider themselves responsible for
their criminality.

Sykes and Matza have argued that delinquents are
not really committed to their acts. Since they
basically do agree with society's norms, they have
to use a number of neutralization techniques in
order to justify their own behavior. One of these
techniques is "denial of responsibility", i.e.,
blaming, for example, bad environment, social
workers, sociological findings, and so on do:

A number of observers have wryly noted that many
delinquents seem to show a surprising awareness of
sociological and psychological explanations for
their behavior and are quick to point out the casual
role of their poor environment. (1957:667)

After this article was written, the argument was
continued in criminological textbooks. Of course, at
strategic moments such as when in court or while
talking to social workers, criminals can use the
technique of denial of responsibility. That they

should view themselves as "more acted upon than acting", as Sykes and Matza argue, does not however seem to be true.

Sykes and Matza's subjects are juvenile delinquents while my sample is composed of older criminals. The respondents here, however, do not come from the class of so-called professional criminals. Many of them belong to a group that vacillates between wishing to go straight and wanting to remain in criminal life - i.e. "drifting", in Matza's (1967) terminology. Furthermore, about a fifth consists of rather young inmates from 17 to 20 years old. The responses from this group to the question above were no different from other group's answers.

When asked why they were criminals, some of the interviewees went so far as to point to their own laziness rather than to lay the blame on their upbringing, society, etc. Glaser (1964) notes the same tendency among some respondents in one of his studies. A large proportion of the highly recidivist or semi-professional criminals even attributed the reason for being unable to quit criminality to "impatient or lazy"; "weak will"; "emotional reaction" or "not deterred".

West's (1982) study provides additional evidence. Only 8% of the 18-year old and 26% of the 21-year old juvenile delinquents gave self-exculpatory (making excuses, denial of responsibility) motives for various kinds of offenses.

Finally, it can be added that when the criminals I interviewed talked about others, they were more inclined to blame their crimes on bad upbringing, etc. than their own. They also described prison as being more detrimental to others than to themselves. "**Some** can't take it so they'll choose isolation just to get away." or "After prison **some** can't even take the bus because they are scared of people." This is probably a general phenomenon: we see our own acts as quite self-determined but others' as the result of external factors.

One could speculate perhaps that claiming

responsibility among criminals is a new phenomenon. In Ødegaard's study of Norwegian recidivists from 1941, however, the interviewed inmates also claimed that they were doing what they wanted to and that they were not led by others. The author also notes that even though most of the men in his sample were dependent on alcohol, only a few of them gave this as the cause of their criminality.

As for **friends**, only 4% of the inmates in my study gave friends as the reason for their criminality. I think this is an offshoot of a rather widely-held norm in our society that you should not blame friends, just as you should not blame your parents. Only 27% of the inmates referred to their **upbringing**, as compared to around two-thirds of the control sample. Ødegaard states the same in his study: even though most of the prisoners came from what he judged as bad homes, only one out of 39 saw this as a cause or an excuse for himself. My study parallels Ødegaard's also in regard to attitudes towards **alcohol and drugs** (narcotics and alcohol both in mine, alcohol only in Ødegaard's) as influencing the interviewees' criminality-drugs are given comparatively low importance. In the taped interviews many of the thieves expressed great contempt towards those who became addicted. The reasoning was that one should be able to use it - not misuse it - or if addicted, quit by oneself. The addicts, on the other hand are more inclined to blame narcotics. As far as alcohol is concerned, only 11% of all inmates gave it as a reason for why they became criminals. As for blaming society, one respondent said, typically:

It's not society's fault that I'm here (in prison) - it's the good money you can earn through crime. That's why I'm here.

One can speculate whether the approach of studying criminality makes a difference when looking at responsibility. It is rather natural, I guess, that those interested in causality has emphasized external factors. Those who have studied crime as work and criminal lifestyles, as for example Shover (1971) and Letkemann (1973) seem however to take into account the criminals' own views of why they are involved in crime. Shover has consequently noted the importance the "good burglar" (i.e., committed and skilled burglars) gives his own self-determination, while Letkemann, who has studied safe-crackers and robbers, makes the following comment:

... the true criminal does not steal against his will (any more than the true square-john goes to his work against his will) ... money factors dictated the temporal routine, but the method of acquiring such money is a matter of perceived choice. (1973:22)

Concomitant with individual responsibility was a dislike of determinism. I think the following result reflects this.

Table 13.   "Once a thief, always a thief."

%	Agree	Disagree	No opinion	Sum	N
Traditional thieves	11	67	22	100	(36)
All inmates	20	53	27	100	(117)

Here again we see that traditional thieves especially deny the deterministic view that there was something forcing them to remain in their present position. This should not necessarily be taken to mean that the respondents believe that they themselves will go straight. Some stated for example that they plan to stop thieving and become fences when they get older.

Most recognized other factors that contributed to their becoming criminals. In the final analysis, however, the respondents stated that it was their own individual choice which led them into criminality.

A good illustration of this reasoning is Martin's

thief in *My Life in Crime* who attributes his entry
into crime to being around wealthy children in
schools whose parents lived by standards that his
own could not afford. He concludes that he got
accustomed to things that were "out of his class".
Later he joined the navy, and travelled a lot and
says he experienced and demanded more than peers of
the same age.

> You take a kid that by the time he's twenty years
> old, he's traveled around ... and seen what a buck
> can do, why he wants more things than the average
> fella would. (1952:8)

However, and this is important, he does not blame
any of these circumstances for his becoming a
criminal:

> I don't blame anyone but myself, I knew much
> better, I always had known right from wrong as far
> as that goes, but that part never stopped me or
> bothered me; it's just been a question of whether
> it's worth while. (Ibid.)

And from another biography, the interviewer asks:

> "What really made you a criminal? Do you know?"
> "This is the point, isn't it, where I should lay
> back in my chair put my feet up on the
> mantelpiece, and say: 'I never had a chance!' But
> it just wouldn't be true. I don't say I've never
> had a chance, because I have, I've plenty of
> chances if I'd wanted to take them. But I never
> did." (Parker and Allerton, 1962:105)

Then he continues to explain some of the processes
involved:

> I'm always afraid of saying circumstances made me
> what I am, because I don't think they did entirely
> at all. Seeing my father, a straight man, getting
> only poverty all through his life ... living in an

environment where nearly everyone I knew was dishonest ... seeing the terrifying dreariness of the
lives of other people who were 'straight' ... not
being able to face working for a living because I
hated the idea of work ... Those were the
circumstances, but they were only part of the
answer. I still think I'd have been a criminal,
whatever they'd been. (Ibid.:106)

Differences between thieves and addicts

As mentioned above, thieves and addicts differed in
their views of causality for becoming criminals. Of
the addicts, 50% said "It is my own fault", while
74% of the thieves took the blame upon themselves.
As we shall see later, these differences remain
constant for other questions concerning taking
individual responsibility. Why then do fewer addicts
look upon themselves as responsible?

Coleman (1975) in his dissertation points out that
addiction in itself does not force people to commit
crimes, as is usually thought. He gives as an
example the American soldiers who became addicted in
Vietnam but give up their addiction once home rather
than resort to crime. Another example is the user
who is just on the fringes of the subculture and
oriented to lighter drug use. Such persons maintain
their contacts with addicts in order to get hold of
drugs. However, they do not want to join them and
they keep the cost of their use low.

Coleman concludes that the street addicts (the
type represented in my study), however, are
encouraged by the general belief that they are
people who desperately need their drugs, resorting
to crime when they must to support their habit. This
expectation arises from the "common knowledge" that
drugs are vital for existence after one has become
addicted and one must commit crimes because drugs
are so expensive. Junkies themselves are caught up
in this self-fulfilling prophecy and thus begin or
continue to commit crime.

I think that the view of drugs as just stated

above can explain to a large part why addicts to a
higher degree than thieves tend to view themselves
as not responsible for their criminality.

Ordinary people's explanation

The current vogue among laymen taken from the social
sciences, as the criminologist Nettler has pointed
out, is to give upbringing, environment, society,
i.e., different social forces, as possible causes
for criminality, instead of putting it on the
individual. In my opinion, his comment on the
tendency today regarding determinism in criminology
is highly accurate:
    It is doubtful that any of us can behave as
consistent determinists. Free will may be an
illusion, and choice too, but most of us regard
these illusions as necessary. At least we seem more
willing to believe that **we decide**, while **others may
be determined.** (1978:204)
    Erskine (1974) reports that most people in an
American poll from 1974 saw upbringing,
neighborhood, parental misguidance, etc. as reasons
for why individuals become criminals. The blue and
white-collar workers in my study shared these views:
the criminals' upbringing was the main cause, while
"friends" and "society" had as large a percentage
for the blue-collar workers as the alternative "it
is their own fault". Among white-collar workers, the
most common explanation was "their upbringing".
Neither drugs or alcohol could really compete among
the alternatives, which is interesting as narcotics
have lately been discussed among researchers and in
the mass media as one of the major causes of
property crime.
    Kellner and Berger (1981) have noted that there is
a growing tendency to interpret sociology in a
general, simplified way as a sort of "scientization"
of everyday life. This type of "sociologism", as the
authors name it, seems to explain the liberal view
the control group took vis-a-vis the reasons why
criminals had become what they were.

Blaming oneself if one gets caught

Among self-respecting criminals, a tendency to blame oneself for getting caught is also quite usual. A safe-cracker, for example, stated that he had got caught "because of the luck of the police and his own carelessness".

This tendency is probably due to two main features. The first is that the structure of their work is highly non-organized and individualistic. Criminal projects are usually planned and carried out alone or in small groups where membership varies. If they have associates, they state that these should be chosen properly - one should know whom to trust. One rule, for example, is never trust an addict. There is thus less opportunity to blame an organization or decisions above one's head, as most of us in conventional work can do. The other factor is that this individualistic performance gives you credit as well as blame. If one does not blame oneself in situations where one has lost, one cannot, to the same extent, take credit and be proud of the successful operations one has carried out.

In criminal work there is thus a need to rely on one's own versatility, on knowing whom to trust, whom to sell to, etc. One small mistake can lead to failure:

Being arrested is usually the result of a combination of wrong moves and bad luck. Picking poor angles, not 'casing' a job thoroughly, engaging a bad partner, failing in skill (not picking a lock or letting goods slip from a coat while shoplifting, etc.), making noise - the list goes on endlessly. (West, 1974:200)

Avoiding these mistakes is up to the individual and he should have planned well enough, have thought things over or be quick to correct his mistakes - otherwise he has failed. On the other hand, some criminals tend to use "the law of averages"[1] to blame their arrests or incarcerations, which is a more deterministic way of looking at it. This means

that sooner or later, if you persist in crime, you
will get caught. The individual's mistakes were
still seen, however, as the primary reason for
getting caught. In analyzing a single crime, his
errors were discussed. These two themes - of
mistakes due to fate or the individual's acts - are
nicely illustrated in an interview by Letkemann.
When questioned whether it is the less successful
who end up doing a lot of time, an inmate replies as
follows:

> No, no - I wouldn't say that ... some of the best
> did a lot of time. But I would think it's just due
> to a person's own fault, or maybe carelessness ...
> Or maybe too much activity. (1973:37)

Too much activity is of course also due to
individualistic decisions. A young man in my study
who vacillated between wanting to go straight and
wanting to keep his lifestyle, declared that if he
chose the second alternative, he would not commit as
many crimes as he previously had done. He had been
"too ambitious" and gave this as the cause for his
now being incarcerated.

Shover interprets the feeling of personal failures
and annoyance with oneself if arrested as due to a
belief in infallibility and technical omnipotence.
The perfect crime **can** be committed since it depends
on careful planning in advance. He describes this
type of belief held by burglars as:

To them a plan of attack possesses a meaning and
value far beyond its instrumental one. Like the
canoes of the Trobianders, they embody a supreme
faith in the inevitable safety and success of the
venture. (1971:120)

One could argue that this faith is instrumental in
itself since both these groups' ventures are to a
high degree built on chance; hence, the faith in
success is needed if the venture is going to get off
the ground at all.

Actually getting caught seems to be a mixture of
strong emotions and consideration of past mistakes:

"When you're arrested, what are your reactions at that moment?"
"I think the first thing's annoyance - with myself. How could I be so stupid to get nicked. What's gone wrong, what have I forgotten, where have I made the mistake?" (Parker and Allerton, 1962:149)

This way of thinking over mistakes can of course be instrumental. One learns the hard way and tries to foresee potentially dangerous elements in advance. Even if these lessons are not always successful:

What caused me to commit crime is the thing I suppose every person that's truthful about it will admit: thinking the next guy got caught, but I won't. I can see his mistake. He shouldn't have done so and so. So I come along and pull a crime and make another mistake. I think within myself, I made that mistake, but when I pull this next trick I will be straight. So I make another mistake. (Jackson, 1972:166)

Taking the consequences: prison

I'll willingly gamble away a third of my life in prison, so long as I can live the way I want for the other two-thirds.[2]

This attitude - being willing to "pay" for being a criminal, one that may seem strange for an outsider - also appeared among my respondents. In an effort to measure how common it was, I posed the question in table 14 to the inmates.

Again, traditional thieves more than other groups claim an individual responsibility. It is obviously easier to accept a prison sentence for the more committed criminals, who to a higher degree than the others see their lifestyle as a choice.

Table 14.   "If you live as a criminal, it's only
             fair that you pay by being in prison
             in a while."

%	Agree	Disagree	No opinion	Sum	N
Traditional					
thieves	59	22	19	100	(37)
Modern					
thieves	42	35	23	100	(43)
Mixed	21	37	42	100	(19)
Addicts	18	50	33	100	(18)

A young committed modern thief who describes the
advantages of crime in terms of free time, etc.,
made the following comment:

> That's how I want to live and it's my own fault
> ... A person can't demand treatment for his
> addiction or his criminality.

And he goes on to say that since he has chosen this
life he is willing to take the "porridge" (slang for
prison).

When asked about the right or wrongness of
prisons, the interviewed thieves usually did not
even elaborate the question but stated simply: "What
should we have instead?" Thus, most took our laws
and punishments for granted, seeing them as
necessary for society in general. As exemplified in
the interview below, most also resented the view of
themselves as "sick" or in need of "help". (Since it
was a group interview, the respondents have been
given numbers.)

> "If someone is supporting himself on crime, is it
> right that he should do time?"
> 1: "Yeah, sure, if you live like this."
> 2: "Yeah, how would it be otherwise? ... You have
> to take the consequences."
> 1: "That's right."
> 2: "But it's different with the cruel crimes, like

rapes and stuff, they should be at a mental hospital."
1: "But sometimes they screw up, placing the wrong person in mental hospitals. This time when I was busted, I was given a mental examination. I told them I didn't need it, it's ridiculous ..."

The interviewee above obviously thinks that being placed in a mental institution is beneath his dignity. His commitment is rather uncomplicated as he considers himself smart: he has supported himself mainly on sickness benefits (i.e. legally) for ten years while doing some "small jobs" on the side. During this time he lived with a non-criminal woman who tried to make him work, which he refused to do. He is also a bit proud of being able to take the prison sentence. "You know, it's not everybody who can take it. It's just certain kinds of people." He can be compared to another man, whom I would label more of an addict, who told me how he tried to cheat the authorities into placing him at a mental hospital because this usually meant shorter sentences.

Coupled with an acceptance of prison sentences is the norm among thieves that one should know in advance what one is gambling with.[3] This is even expressed in statements about those who use heroin. "They knew what they were getting into and I don't like this thing of feeling sorry for them. Feeling sorry, feeling sorry, it's always that crap," as a young self-righteous thief expressed it.

For the committed criminals, prison sentences can be seen as an occupational hazard and thus made less dramatic. One should not oversimplify, of course. Even those who saw it in this way talked about the problems of imprisonment, reflecting on the possibility of spending so much time in prison that their criminality in the end would not be worth it. But quite a few saw it as a part of their life that even had certain advantages: one met old friends, got regular meals, etc.

One respondent said that he did not even get upset

any more when arrested, "It's just packing my things
and then I'm in again for a while. I don't count
days and after a while I'm out again. It really
doesn't bother me anymore." As far as I could judge,
this man had not become institutionalized,[4] so that
explanation does not seem to be valid. Besides, he
had spent quite a long time outside between
sentences and had a wife whom he cared for. In
biographies of criminals we can find the same
undramatic attitudes towards prison sentences,
defined as occupational hazards:

> If you're a criminal, what's the alternative to
> the risk of going to prison? Coal-miners don't
> spend their time worrying about the fact that they
> might get killed by a fall at the coal-face
> either. Prison's an occupational risk, that's all.
> (Parker and Allerton, 1962:88)

Another thief when talking about leaving prison,
relates to it in a similar way:

> It was hardly a unique situation. In fact, these
> exits and entrances were the occupational hazards
> of my chosen trade. (MacKenzie, 1955:7)

The process of becoming a committed criminal is
probably further facilitated after experiencing, as
some stated they did, that prison was not as bad as
they had thought before being there. Both Shover
(1971) and West (1974) as well point out that some
of the interviewed thieves in their studies saw
their first prison sentence in this light.

Going legal

Table 15.   "If someone wants to go straight and
            succeeds in doing so, what would you
            think of as a primary cause for this?"

%	All inmates	Control group
Work and housing	41	27
Meeting a girl or starting a family	61	20
That they really want to quit	66	87
To get away from old friends	32	30
N	(137)	(192)

Note: The respondents gave more than one answer to
this question. The same is the case in the
next table.

Table 16.   "If someone wants to quit drugs and
            succeeds in doing so, what would you
            think of as the primary cause for
            this?"

%	All inmates	Control group
Work and housing	41	22
Meeting a girl or starting a family	40	16
That they really want to quit	83	87
To get away from old friends	36	42
N	(131)	(191)

Inmates judge their own self-determination as one of
the most important factors in quitting both
criminality and drugs. The control group agrees;
this is somewhat contrary to their belief as to the
sources of criminality. The inmates believe that the

individual's wish to quit influence addicts more
than thieves. I think this might be due to the fact
that thieves do not think that they themselves have
personal problems; their main reason for wanting to
quit is more often instrumental or for the sake of
others.

Many in my sample state that they have had chances
to go straight but they have rejected them. A former
old thief was quite upset because he believed that
one really got a lot of help if one **wanted** to go
legal. The problem was that so few of them really
wished to. Irwin notes the same individualistic
orientation towards going straight in his interviews
with convicts about to be released:

Most of them expressed the belief that making it
is up to the individual, and now that they had
decided to try to make it their chances were very
good. Most who came back, they believed, don't want
to make it. (1970:112)

Inmates are often more optimistic about their own
chances of making it when they came out, more
pessimistic concerning other inmates' chances.[5] This
might be due to several things. One is that inmates
who state that they want to go straight can be
ridiculed. Such an atmosphere probably leads to
beliefs that others do not really want to quit. My
interviews with former criminals confirmed that a
decision or wish to quit is not something one talks
too much about in prison.

An individualistic optimism might also be
necessary if an inmate intends to make it legally.
In an article about future orientation, delinquents
felt that their futures depended on their own
actions to a higher degree than did non-delinquents.
The authors' interpretation of the results seems
highly plausible:

One may also assume that expectation of internal
control may reflect the belief of institutionalized
delinquents that following release they will have to
confront reintegration into society without much
help from others. The strictly regulated time in
prison being over, they will have to plan and be

responsible for themselves. (Trommsdorff and Lamm, 1980:271)

The perspective of seeing future developments as due to one's own acts can thus be seen as both realistic and instrumental.

What one thinks about the importance of one's own efforts can in part be measured through questions of what type of work the inmates wanted after they got out of prison (table 17). Those who specified which type they wanted were then asked if they thought they would get it:

Table 17.   "Do you think you will work with any of
             these jobs when you get out?"

%	Inmates
Yes, because I	
made a decision	33
have the education	14
worked with that before	36
have contacts	17
Total number (yes answer):	82
No, because	
no one wants to hire	
a former inmate	7
too much unemployment	10
lack of education	15
can not "take" a job or	
do not really want a job	8
Total number (no answer):	31
Have not answered the question	8
The percentage is based on	
the total of those who	
indicated that they wanted	
some type of work	121

Note: More than one alternative has been given so
         the sums can not be added. A few gave both yes
         answers and no answers.

The alternatives were formulated as yes-because and no-because alternatives, and were posed in such a way as to see what emphasis the inmates put on instrumental reasons of a practical nature and to what extent they were optimistic about getting a job as a result of their own efforts. The no-alternatives, taken from arguments about the difficulties that inmates had in getting jobs, were provided by the inmates themselves in taped interviews and or referred to in criminological literature.

The fact that one had made a decision was seen as important by as many as a third of those who said they wanted a job.

Relatively few believed that they would not get the job they wanted. The most common no-answer is "because I do not have the education", which is in line with the fact that this group has a generally lower education than the rest of the population. Some had also mentioned jobs as "social worker", "photographer", etc., where it was evident that they did not have the necessary specialized education. In those cases, of course, difficulties in finding the job were not due to a general low education. Of interest for this study, however, is the fact that relatively few stated "no one wants to hire a former inmate", a response in keeping with the "denial of responsibility" answer. One should also remember in this context that many inmates state that it is nice if you can avoid work altogether:

Table 18.   "It's nice if you can avoid work."

%	Agree	Disagree	No opinion	Sum	N
All inmates	35	47	18	100	(110)
Control group	7	87	6	100	(198)

This result is consistent with Bondeson's (1974), where one-third of the interviewed inmates stated that they did not want a regular job after their time was up. According to her, the reasons were that they dislike work after being in prison or that they consider their opportunities for getting a job as

bad. I, on the other hand, interpret these results
as indicating rather a truthful account of their
attitudes - that they simply prefer not to work, at
least not for the time being and in the kind of work
available to them. In order to motivate the inmates
to participate when I presented my questionnaire, I
said something like, "It is important to know what
type of work you want to have after you are
released." A few laughed and said, "No one here
wants a job, forget about that." Even if this is not
true of everyone, it is important to recognize that
there is not a general consensus among criminals
that striving to acquire a legal job is something
worthwhile.

Reaction against therapy

Since criminals see both getting in and getting out
of crime largely their own decision, getting
"therapy" seems quite peculiar to them.
   Several scholars have also pointed out how
committed criminals react towards therapy. Nettler
(1978) even refers to "the tyranny of therapy".
Cressey (1978) emphasizes the importance of self as
one of the few things left during incarceration.
Irwin (1970) describes inmates' hostility towards
explanations in line with an emotional disturbance
model (a non-responsible model) to account for
criminality. A quote from an autobiography is
illustrative:

   For me there was never any escape from group
   therapy, since I was always quite candid in
   admitting that I was a thief because I had a
   marked aversion to the 40-hour week. This didn't
   go over at all well in a system geared to the
   premise that a thief is never a thief through
   preference, but through the workings of a warped
   id. Nature's abhorance of a vacuum, I tell you, is
   a nothing compared to the psychologist's loathing
   of a simple and direct explanation. (MacIsaacs,
   1968:69)

Treatment or therapy, however, not only blames the mental state but, more commonly, one's background. Degrading your background and especially your family, who are usually the most important of the significiant others, is in a way degrading you. This helps to explain the aversion to outsiders trying to lay the blame for one's criminality on one's upbringing.

Therapy can also be used as a type of "value imperialism" by defining values of the actor as right or wrong - not the specific acts or behaviors according to formal ground such as breaking the law. Criminals often have a rich source of stories about do-gooders trying to educate them about "right attitudes", which they interpret as a way of getting them to be more like their teachers. This lack of respect for different values is related by Allerton in a typical conversation (as he sees it) with one of these do-gooders (psychiatrists, priests, prison visitors, welfare workers, etc.):

"Now do you really think, honestly, that this keeping on going back to prison all the time is worth it? (Of course they don't mean 'honestly' at all. When I say honestly that I do, they can't believe I mean it.)."
"But you don't want to spend all your life in prison, do you?"
"No."
"Well, then ... "
"I'm not going to spend all my life in prison. I've only spent a third of it there, up to now. You said 'all'."
"All right, then, a third - do you think that's worth it?"
"Yes."
...
"Haven't you any sense of responsibility, or desire for security?"
"No."
"Don't you want to be like other people and work

for your living?"
"No." (Parker and Allerton, 1962:141-42)

Possible reasons for Thieves' claiming resposibility

Why then is individual responsibility seen as being so important? Part of the explanation can be found in criminals' self-images - of being grown-ups (even while still young), as "real men" and as action-seekers. Furthermore, analyzing them as marginal men gives us yet another clue and finally individualism of this kind can be seen as functional to the group.

Age

Klockars (1974) describes how the fence Vincent whom he studied saw the people buying from and selling to him as being grown-up people who made their own decisions. Therefore he had no remorse or feelings of guilt. Furthermore, he viewed his own life with a similar sense of individual resposibility.

In very much the same way, the respondents in my study saw age as important in the sense that being a grown-up implies making decisions by oneself. When you are grown-up, you no longer have any excuses to fall back on.

Even the most unfortunate case in my opinion among those I interviewed claimed that after he had grown up, he was the one responsible for continuing with crime. He was rather atypical from the rest of the population, and was a "perfect" example of a disastrous background and upbringing: his parents were alcoholics, his father beat him and he had been at bad foster homes, and at an old-fashioned mental hospital where they had put a straight-jacket on him at the age of twelve. My sympathetic remark after hearing the whole story was: "Well, then it's quite natural to become defiant?" His reply is interesting in the present context:

"Well, yeah, but in later years I've chosen this

life."
"You've chosen it yourself?"
"Yes I have. I'm so old now that I know what I'm doing ... but at that age (as an adolescent) one did not think too much."

This young man wanted to go straight but thought he might be too old: he was twenty-four. Another young man in his early twenties also saw himself making a decision now about his criminality "because when you were young, you were 'super criminal' but then society taught you and said, 'Naughty boy, that's not how to behave'. And at that point you learned and chose." And still another young man thought that one was only influenced by friends while young:

"No one drags me into anything if I don't want it."
"But when you were younger?"
"Yeah, but when you were young, you believed in those who were older and wanted to live up to their ... It's easy to cheat you before you've got your own experiences. But then at last you're on your own feet, then you don't care about what others think. If others won't accept me as I am, then I don't care because you can't change just in order to satisfy others. And if you hold a hard line you'll be more respected."

Quite a few of the respondents talked about how they had been independent very early. "Too early", said some. Criminals might be extreme in this way but there is probably a general class difference operating here. In Persson and Dahlgren's (1975) book on youth in Sweden, it is reported that 8% of ten and twelve-year olds do not wish to leave their childhood. This group consists mainly of children from the upper class. Gans (1962) on the other hand describes the lower class Italian children he studied as miniature grown-ups. Werthman (1969) describes a demand for independence and a wish to be taken seriously (not as children) as typical for the delinquent children and youth that he has studied. Finally B-E Andersson's (1982) recent study of ordinary young people in Sweden can be referred to, in which (rather amazingly) only a quarter of 20 and 21-year olds saw themselves as grown-ups. At the age of 23, this had increased to 60%. Even though I do not have any statistical evidence from criminals in this matter, I am rather sure the percentage would have been higher than that of these studied young people.

Manliness

Many of the thieves struck me as quite "macho"-directed. If this is the case, a denial of responsibility would be considered unmanly.
One of the traditional roles of the man has been that of the provider and the financial organizer. In the tape-recorded interviews many thieves stated, "I don't want my wife to work, that's the man's business." The following result from the questionnaire confirms that this is a more common attitude among thieves than the other groups.

Table 19. "In my opinion the man is the one who should support the family."

%	Agree	Disagree	No opinion	Sum	N
Traditional thieves	42	28	31	100	(37)
Addicts	17	45	39	100	(19)
Control group	18	60	22	100	(198)

Traditional thieves share this quite old-fashioned ideal of manliness to a large extent. They differ a lot from the response of the control sample, which much more reflect the typical view in Sweden of today where most women work.

Inmates on the whole, and especially thieves, also agreed to a higher extent than the control group to the statement "A man ought to put the interest of

his wife and children above his own". Fifty-nine
percent of the thieves agreed compared to 24% of the
"average guys".

Being a provider does not, however, necessarily
mean taking care of a woman through legal means of
support. An older thief told me that the first thing
he said to his wife when she worried about their
finances was, "Daddy'll take care of that",
whereafter he went out and stole. And from an
American biography, we learn why prostitutes like
thieves:

> Prostitutes are attracted by a thief. For one
> thing he is a provider and they like that.
> (Chambliss and King, 1972:14)

In the table above, addicts differed from thieves in
not thinking it is the man's responsibility to
support his family. For those addicts who passed
through the stages of the hippie movement and its
philosophy, manliness in this sense is clearly
irrelevant if not negative.

Inmates did not differ among themselves in their
general attitude towards taking an individualistic
responsibility for having bad finances.

Table 20.   "You have yourself to blame if your
              finances are bad."

%	Agree	Disagree	No opinion	Sum	N
All inmates	52	28	21	100	(114)
SIFO	52	29	19	100	(125)

Furthermore, inmates are strikingly similar to
conventional people. This is interesting because one
of the current topics discussed among social workers
and criminologists is that criminals do not have a
fair chance for readjustment because of their debts
and bad finances in general when they get out of
prison. Criminals could have taken the opportunity
to declare that because of all kinds of unhappy,

unintended circumstances such as doing foolish things while on drugs, being drunk, unhappy etc. they had not been in control of their economy. This, however, most of them did not do, as is seen in table 20.

Although thieves and addicts did not differ on this question, there does seem to be a difference between them: addicts cannot be describes as "providers" as they "provide" for themselves only, in more or less socially acceptable ways. Those who do not are degraded as "junkies" according to an American study:

On the block, there is a distinction between an addict and a junkie. An addict has pride. A junkie will stoop to anything to support his habit: "He'll hustle his own sister. That's disgusting ... I feel that if you have a habit, support it ... Be a man about it ... If you go to steal, go steal. It's a job like any other job. You make faster money, and you deprive people of other things, but it's a job." ... They require certain skills and stealing is one of them. (Burnham, 1970:158)

In *Portraits from a Shooting Gallery*, Fiddle also notes that addicts have "an individualism of their own".[6]

If one talks long enough to addicts, one discovers that they do have an individualism of their own ... they put down the man who is a beggar, who does not forage his own heroin. Secondly, an addict will argue that he is "responsible" for keeping up his habit. That is to say, he will go out and steal, and so on, and do all the things a good hustler would do in order to get the money he needs to support himself. (1967:49)

The view that each should take care of his own financial situation sometimes fosters a rather condescending attitude towards those who fail in this: Letkemann presents an armed robber's attitude towards the "young punks". In contrast to "those who get into serious crime", he referred to those who are unsuccessful - "They don't pull their own weight either working, stealing or anything". This

resembles the inmates' description of prison guards
as being "too lazy to work and too yellow to steal".
(1973:24)

In line with this attitude is the statement about
the poor made by an older man in my study, who
himself looked a bit worn: "I feel sorry for them."
Obviously he did not see himself as belonging to
that group. This condescending attitude can
sometimes become a sort of impatience with those who
accept their poverty. After having committed a
burglary in a rich aristocrat's house, this thief
says:

> I remember after I'd come out I passed an old man
> in rags, standing on the street-corner scraping at
> a violin to try and earn himself a few coppers,
> and I thought: you mug, why don't you go in there
> and at least get yourself a good sleep in one of
> his Lordship's unused beds for a night. (Parker
> and Allerton, 1962:89)

With the background of criminals' wanting to take
care of their own finances, I posed a question about
the attitude to social welfare.

Table 21.   "It's okay to take social welfare."

%	Agree	Disagree	No opinion	Sum	N
Traditional thieves	46	41	14	100	(37)
Addicts	65	18	18	100	(17)
Control group	27	45	28	100	(198)

Inmates are more inclined to see social welfare as
"okay", but traditional thieves hold a more
individualistic view concerning coping with one's
own finances. They also are closer to the control
group than to the addicts: as many of them actually
disagreed to social welfare as of the control
sample.

I think the number of thieves who morally disagree

might be a bit higher than indicated due to the fact
that they actually have been in situations where
they had to ask for social welfare money. An
indication of this is that the "no opinion"
alternative is less frequently chosen by inmates
while 28% of the control group chosen that
alternative. Judging from the taped interviews, a
more ideal attitude seemed to be exemplified in this
statement of an older thief:

> I don't see myself as having any duties towards
> society, therefore I don't think I have any rights
> either.

Similarly, Letkemann reports on a criminal who would
rather choose crime than "... collect social welfare
and be a nuisance for the rest of my life."
(1973:22)

There seems to be a difference here between the
group norms of thieves and those of addicts. To
simplify a bit, one could say that for thieves it
was degrading to take social welfare when one could
steal, while for addicts, manipulating the social
workers could be something to be proud of and brag
about among friends.

The norms among traditional thieves concerning
supporting oneself are in line with their view of
success in the light of the American Dream.

Table 22. "It is up to you whether you will
succeed or not, everyone is his own
fortune-maker."

%	Agree	Disagree	No opinion	Sum	N
Traditional thieves	76	8	16	100	(37)
All inmates	61	19	20	100	(129)
Blue-collar workers	51	26	23	100	(103)
White-collar workers	71	14	15	100	(93)

It is interesting that the traditional thief group is closer to the white-collar group than to the blue-collar one although its social background more closely resembles that of the latter. Here, I think it is important to note that the white-collar workers come from a private company and not a public organization. The group includes quite a large percentage of people placed in leading positions. That is, the group is not typical for a normal Swedish white-collar sample and might be more "achievement-oriented".

Finally yet another expression of manly ideals is the attitude towards doing military service. Traditional thieves did not appreciate those who refuse to 'go in' (military service is compulsory in Sweden) - even more so in fact than the control sample from SIFO.

Table 23.   "The refusal to carry arms and go to war is admirable."

%	Agree	Disagree	No opinion	Sum	N
Traditional thieves	23	66	11	100	(35)
Modern thieves	40	41	19	100	(42)
Mixed	22	28	50	100	(18)
Addicts	61	11	29	100	(18)
SIFO	24	53	23	100	(125)

The questions above do not of course provide sufficient information for a thorough examination of what manliness is or is perceived to be, but may illustrate how male thieves tend to see themselves as "real men". And it can further be viewed as influencing this group in valuing responsibility since the two concepts are so closely connected in our civilization. Finally it must be emphazised that the questions refer to values and views, not to actual behavior. If one were to measure the percentage of thieves who actually do serve in the

military, my guess is that it would be lower than
that of the non-thieves. The same can probably be
said for the items concerning who is to support the
family. When they answered the questionnaire, some
initially agreed that this was the man's business
but after a while they changed their answers because
they acknowledged the fact that when they were in
prison, their girl friends or wives were really
doing it.

Action-seekers

The fact that criminals consider themselves as "men-
of-action" also inclined them to claim an
individualistic responsiblity. According to Goffman
people in fateful action-oriented occupations
generally tend to perceive these as wilful
undertakings:

   Those with faithful duties sometimes hold
themselves to be self-respecting men who aren't
afraid to put themselves on the line ... They have
more or less secret contempt for those with safe and
secure jobs who need never face real tests of
themselves. They claim they are not only willing to
remain in jobs full of opportunity and risk, but
have deliberately sought out this environment,
declining to accept safe alternatives, being able,
willing, and even inclined to live in a challenge.
(1967:182)

   A typical group of action-seekers are gamblers.
Many criminals see themselves as gamblers, and life
itself as a game to be played with gains and
losses.[7] The interviewees were asked to choose one
of the statements in table 24 as most representative
of their life philosophy.

   As seen in the table, criminals attribute less to
fate than blue-collar workers do. Gambling on the
other hand is the most common alternative for them.
It should be remembered, that this is opposite to
fate in that it is something that concerns decisions
made by the actor.

Table 24.   **Game:** "Life is like a game where one can win or lose."

Fate: "Life goes on without our being able to do much about it, just take one day at a time."

Planning: "In general, one can plan one's life, at least in the long run."

%	Game	Fate	Planning	Sum	N
Traditional thieves	45	24	32	100	(38)
Addicts	24	29	47	100	(17)
All inmates	40	28	32	100	(139)
Blue-collar workers	17	30	54	100	(101)
White-collar workers	17	14	69	100	(93)

Life in general, is viewed quite differently from the perspective of the criminal than from that of the ordinary person. A young "modern thief":

> You see, we are gamblers, we who're here (in prison). Most addicts and thieves are. We play with our lives as stakes.

And then he goes on to say that this is reflected in the fact that they actually do gamble concretely, i.e., poker, slotmachines, etc. One way of dealing with fatefulness as described by Goffman is to ascribe the outcome of actions as due to fate. The results above are interesting in that criminals do not seem to consider fate as a vital determinant in life - not more than the blue-collar group.[8] This view is important in that criminals are not passively awaiting the outcome of fate, even if they do not see life as something that one can carefully plan, but something one can gamble with - win or lose. The following statement illustrates how this gambling is considered voluntary. An older versatile man who has been engaged in "everything", smuggling, dealing, having a legal business ...

Life is a gamble, you can't predict everything in detail. You make a drawing sort of, and then the run starts so to say and after that you'll just have to see how it works out ... I don't really like planning.

Chance-taking is also something that is appreciated. A young thief:

"Do you like to take chances?"
"Yeah, absolutely."
"Why?"
"Well ... it's excitement and it can pay off."

This is an attitude that is not self-evident among all groups: almost half of the inmate group as compared to a quarter of the SIFO sample stated that they appreciated chance-taking. (See table 46)
    A few quotes to illustrate how crime as opposed to life in general can be perceived as gambling and chance-taking. An older man calling himself a jack-of-all-trades, whose main line is being a con man:

"Have you sometimes reasoned like 'Okay, I'm committing crimes and I know they're punishable, but I'll take that?'"
"I have reasoned like that but then I've been thinking like I don't give a damn. I can get busted but I might make it as well, it's a fifty-fifty chance."
"Is it worth taking that risk?"
"Yeah! If you don't wanna work ... if you don't take a chance you won't get anything."

If you lose the game it is **the individual** who blows it - he usually does not attribute the losses to the insecurity in the game itself, which would be the most likely according to common sense. The implication according to Goffman is that neither the possession of the stake nor the loss was particularly justified or legitimate. Even if one's loss is bad for one's self-image, one can fairly easily excuse oneself for making it. This is probably the basis for being able to state "I blew it", i.e., the non-seriousness in the midst of serious gambling - which according to Simmel (1971) is typical for the experience of adventure.

Criminals can actually be seen as not "serious", i.e. not seriously planning a future in crime. Most of them are committed **for a while** and a criminal lifestyle can thus be seen as an adventure - at least when they are young.[9] Only about a fifth in my study saw it as possible in the long run to support oneself on crime. Thus, when they gamble and lose in crime their loss will not be total in the sense of destroying a whole career planned for a life-time.

Goffman also points to the connection between action and character. One character trait is courage. This is exemplified by a willingness to submit to the rules of the game and by carrying the gain or loss with grace. The same mechanism seems to be involved in the righteous criminal's willingness to "pay" with a sentence if his luck or skills betray him. The code of the committed thief demands that he has already weighed the risks of what he is involved in. Subsequently the individual should be prepared to take the consequences.

> There is little sympathy for the man who reacts with shock and weakness of character when arrested and sentenced to prison ... In the prisons of Illinois too oft-repeated admonitions are sure to greet the man who complains of his adversity. **"If you wanna' play, you gotta' pay"**; and **"if you can't do the time, don't do the crime"**. (Shover, 1971:117)(my emphasis)

This contempt towards those who "can't take it" is, I think based on the feelings expressed by those who view themselves as action - seekers who voluntarily seek action and can handle its possible drawbacks.

Blaming one's act on someone else means that you withdraw this positive self-image. The positive value that was put on self-determination was seen in the way the interviewed thieves talked about addicts. They did not refer to the fact that someone used drugs or even that they were addicted to drugs; rather, addicts were those who lacked moral strength of "character". A "righteous" thief:

> If a man is going to use dope I look at that like anything else: use it, and use as much discretion as possible. But when you get a pop, don't go screaming about everybody else is a damn fool or they're square because they're persecuting you for using it. Just say 'I done used it, I got caught, it's against the laws of society and conventional-thinking people, so now I got to serve the consequences', go pay'em. (Jackson, 1972:165)

That one should not fuss about one's drug use was something most of the " righteous criminals" in this study also emphasized. Those who did not employ discretion while using drugs in prison, for example, were looked down upon. A young man who sees himself as a thief, but who has tried different types of drugs and been addicted to amphetamine is thus quite upset about addicts' tendencies to lose self-control. Both thieves and addicts should "accept what they are" and keep their dignity.

> Okay, even if you're an addict you should keep your human dignity and not sell out like they do. It's actually happened that I've bought a color TV at the time when you got good money for them from one of them and give him **one** capsule just so that he could get the drug inside him ... And that's an uncontrolled addict, see ... Well, he should see to it that he gets straight in his head again and not sell out like that ... The years I used drugs I never felt I had to get it, **had to,** you know. Not on uppers. Okay the guy shooting, he can't ... Well, I've taken that as well and I don't like it.

I think the junkie is an idiot. I won't give you
one penny for someone like that because he knows
that if he takes the drug he'll get hooked
physically.

The moral is thus that even though you might get
hooked, you should have enough sense to get yourself
straight if you use uppers. If one starts to use
heroin, the blame is totally the individual's,
knowing the danger of the drug. Flirting with drugs
can however be seen as getting involved in "fateful
situations". These situations can then be seen as
chances for displaying character. Going through a
chancy situation, which people involved in action
often view as being undertaken voluntarily as seen
above, is also an opportunity to display pride. It
is precisely this that is considered lacking in
addicts. The true criminals, on the other hand, take
advantage of situations "when the chips are down",
e.g., when being arrested.
    The type of prison one has been to can also serve
as a proof of manhood -having done time at a tough
prison helps you become a "right guy". Similarily,
the type of punishment one has received can function
in the same way. Allerton - a righteous thief - was
asked if bringing back "the cat" (a harsh form of
punishment no longer in use in Britain) would change
the attitudes toward punishment among criminals. He
replied that it would not. The ones he knew who had
received that punishment only became more vicious
and

... in certain cases it's increased their standing
in the criminal world, they're quite proud of it
and look on themselves like heroes, like - well,
fighter pilots in the battle of Britain, something
of that sort. (Parker and Allerton, 1962:102)

Marginal man

The concept of marginal man was first developed by
Park. He saw, for example, the Jew in modern society

as "... a man on the margin of two cultures and two societies ..." (1950:354). Stonequist developed the concept in his book *The Marginal Man* where he dealt with the problems of being 'inbetween' as was the case for the mulatto or the educated blacks. Both authors, however, according to Shibutani (1961), over-emphasized the problems and personal difficulties connected with a marginal position. Other types of marginality have subsequently been described, such as the foreman, the military chaplain, the chiropractor and the Japanese-Americans. Many of these studies have reported that the holders of these positions have revealed few serious inner conflicts.

Even though criminals are not usually labelled as "marginal men", I think a lot of them can be described as such. Seeing them as marginal men may help to explain both why criminals often argue with emphasis that they themselves have chosen their life and why they state a responsibility for this:

People who occupy a marginal status are continually confronted with the necessity of forming moral judgement. Situations that would be routine for other people call for choice, often a choice between different conceptions of what is right. (Shibutani, 1961:578)

In many ways criminals can be seen as marginal men. In the first place, even those who appear highly committed to their criminal life **for the moment** had tried at one point or another to lead a straight life. Sixty-one percent stated that they had lived a square life.[10] Few wanted their children to live like they had done. A fifth said they usually socialized with their family, which was described as "straight", and a third with ordinary people, when they were out of prison. The majority of the group had furthermore mainly supported themselves through legitimate work.[11]

Many of the interviewees also wanted to quit their criminal life at some point in the future - even if they did not want a job that was seen as dull. The main reason as to why they wanted to quit was for

their parents' or wife and children's sake. A further example, as I see it, of marginality is that a
fourth of the inmates stated that those who managed
to live like the squares but supported themselves by
crime were appreciated and respected.

All this indicates that criminals do not live in a
closed culture where norms are taken for granted.
This can of course be difficult at times - but not
necessarily as Park and Stonequist described it. The
strain might result more from practical considerations. Some said, for example, that it was hard to
change language when one came out. Others did not
want to associate with criminals on the outside
because it was like talking "shop talk" all the
time. Besides they meant that criminals often have
problems and they had enough of this inside. The
most extreme example I heard of someone being in a
marginal position was a safe-cracker who at one time
had had a building firm of his own with thirteen
employees. To manage the firm's finances he had to
be out stealing at nights.

The marginal position that criminals occupy may
cause choices to be made with a **higher degree of
awareness** than most of us have to use in our lives
where a larger number of decisions are taken for
granted. The criminal life is also continuously
questioned by others. If criminals are to continue,
they are more or less forced to explain this to
themselves or others, something most of us in
conventional work need not do.

Nor does it seem any longer the case in Sweden
that a criminal gets socialized into the criminal
world through neighborhood associates,[12] etc. which
would provide the individual criminal with a taken-
for-granted "safety net" which would make conscious
decisions unnecessary since activities would not be
questioned by him or by those around him.

Another circumstance that caused a higher
awareness of choice is that one knows that both
types of lives have drawbacks. Going straight means
a disinvestment of skills and contacts and requires
a lot of new learning, making of new contacts, new

routines, and so on, which adds up to a lot of individual efforts with few ready-made channels smoothing the way: for example the decision to keep old friends away, resisting the temptation of offers to be in on a scheme, disciplining oneself to new routines budgeting one's time and money, getting to know new people, maybe concealing one's past, etc. All those things are known to most criminals and thus they know at least the difficulties on this alternative road. Some seem to make the choice then to continue even if they are attracted in some respects to living a life where they do not support themselves by crime. But this, then, also calls for a decision. In the respect described above, crime as a lifestyle is living in a marginal world.

Positive functions for the group

The jazz musician Art Pepper, who for a while supported his drug habit by stealing, tells about an occasion when he and two other, more experienced, thieves were dividing the take after a burglary:

> We counted up the money. They were going to throw the checks away but I said, 'No, let me have them.' They said,'You know you've got to be awfully careful. ...And if anything happens, that's **you**. Period.' I said,'I know that. You don't have to worry about me.' They said, 'Well, you've been in prison. You know what it's all about.' (1979:233)

The norm of not ratting and taking care of oneself is of course due to group necessity. If this norm did not exist, our prisons would be even more overcrowded.[13] The norms among thieves also includes knowing what one is doing in advance - risks should be calculated and help from others is not be expected. Einstadter (1969) reports for example about one infor mant who said, when asked about obligations towards members in a gang who were arrested, that one does not go into armed robbery blind to the risks and if caught, one should be prepared to handle the situation on one's own and accept the consequences.

Secondly, as was pointed out earlier, the individual living as a criminal, has little choice other than to rely on his own resources. This is usually the case after he leaves prison. Contrary to most ordinary people who, for example, leave a hospital and who have a family and a job, waiting, the former inmate does not have this type of safety net. His own efforts will make or break him - in crime or otherwise. It would also be hazardous if criminals relied too much on each other. If one is escaping and hiding out with others, for example, one will make the place "hot".

Letkemann (1973) attributes the norm of "doing your own time" to the fact that inmates are not in a position to offer each other much help.[14] Another reason for the rather hard attitude is that they have enough problems of their own without taking on someone else's.

As a final comment to this chapter, it should be added that 'taking responsibility' has, for criminals, a special connotation. It implies an expressiveness; it is - at least partly - used as a means of showing that one is a man who stands up for his action. In this sense it is different from that which refers to taking on long-term commitments concerning a family or a job, which is perhaps the meaning we usually attach to responsibility.

6
TIME-PERSPECTIVES

... the idea of time and its division is to a great degree a **social convention.** These divisions into various periods are reflections of **social rhythms of activities;** these are their bases. (Sorokin, 1943:184)

According to Aubert (1979), the importance of time for social action is seldom made explicit in sociological analysis. Perhaps this neglect is due to the fact that most groups conceive time in the same manner, i.e., in our industrial society, time is clock time (Horton 1977).

Maybe this is why criminologists have so often interpreted an orientation to the present as a dominant feature of the criminal lifestyle. In this view lies an implicit understanding of criminals as not being oriented to the future in their way of acting. The picture given is therefore one in which individuals live for the moment without thinking of tomorrow - in contrast to those who are well adjusted and have a more responsible attitude towards their future. This seems to spring from the fact that future orientation is equated with long-run goals, as has been the case in most deferred gratification discussions.

This reasoning can be criticized in two ways.

Firstly, it contains some rather unclear value-judgements and, secondly, it gives a misleading view of how criminals actually experience their acts in relation to their future consequences.

The conventional view

Some quotations from classic criminological literature will serve to demonstrate the dominant view of traditional criminals as being hedonistic, irresponsible and having a "live-for-the-moment" attitude towards life.

Cohen is probably one of the best examples of this view in his description of juveniles engaged in non-utilitarian delinquency: "There is little interest in long-run goals, in planning activities and budgeting time ..." (1960:30). His description of "shortrun hedonism" is similar to the picture Matza and Sykes (1961) gave of juvenile delinquents as concentrating on leisure and being "big-time spenders".

In some of the most famous descriptions of different criminal subcultures we get the same picture of present orientation. Maurer writes that a pickpocket:

... lives very intensively in the present. The past and the future are alike unimportant in his thinking, though he may derive much pleasure from reminiscing over past experiences, and likewise daydream grandly about his prosperity in the future. (1955:24)

The same theme of refusing to plan or even think about the future, unless it is daydreaming about the "big score" runs through Sutherland's (1937) famous book about the professional thief.

According to Maurer and Sutherland this inability to consider the future is due to its being seen as more or less hopeless. Sooner or later criminals will have to serve a prison sentence and in addition they are aware of their limited opportunities in the conventional world. As a group solution, says Sutherland, all serious discussion about the future is abandoned - instead one jokes about it and has a "bravado attitude".

The realism in being a spendtrift

As is discussed further on in this book, the inmates described their attitude towards money by the expression "easy come, easy go". Being a spendthrift is often considered as expressing the fact that individuals live for the moment instead of planning for the future.

For criminals this behavior could instead be seen as quite rational. A statement by a former addict can serve as an example of behavior that might appear as hedonistic and oriented towards the present but which is not:

"Sometimes you'll have things going for you so that you can set yourself up with an apartment and furniture. You buy furniture because you need it and during that time you can afford to do it ... what I can't afford is to wait until next week because by that time I might be broke or in prison ..."
"You mean you have to take advantage of your opportunities?"
"You've got to act fast when you've got money, you know."

In the middle class especially, money is spent on permanent things such as houses, education that leads to a degree, etc. The consequence of this is that once these things are planned for and bought, time is spent mainly on the care and development of these investments rather than on the consideration of other alternatives. In the criminal world on the other hand, some investments that are seen as "sensible", such as a buying a house, are just not possible since there is no way to legally account for how they have been able to buy them. Spending on more transient things is thus also in this perspective a rational behavior.

Availability

"Making it" on the street requires constant
orientation to unpredictable opportunities and
readiness to make quick decisions concerning the
expected value of proposed schemes. (Goffman,
1967:173)

As used above, availability means that criminals
need to be present in order to make use of
opportunities that they cannot predict - a sort of
constant preparedness to take advantage of
situations.

Hanging around

"Hanging around" in bars, apartments, parks, etc.,
is required if criminals are to support themselves
in their world and hence is not just a sign of being
oriented to the present. It is also an expression of
criminals needing more manipulative zones in their
everyday life.[1]
The same mechanism is involved in the actions of
groups such as the dance musicians described by
Becker (1966). The dependable musician is the one
who is readily available and accepts any offers he
gets to play. For record companies employees or
those engaged in writing about music it might be
equally important to "hang around" clubs picking up
new trends and potential "stars of tomorrow". The
same characteristic - making oneself sociably
accessible - can be seen in such groups as free-
lancers in the worlds of theatre, fashion, etc.
Some of the former addicts who had worked as
pushers actually complained about how boring it was
to hang around parks and squares waiting for
customers to show up. But this was necessary for
many of them. One reason could be that they were not
sufficiently established to have people calling them
up but instead had to make themselves accessible to
the customers. This resembles the waiting and

hanging out in strategic places that prostitutes who are not working in massage parlors or the like have to engage in.[2] Obviously "hanging around" in such circumstances is not a sign of a "happy-go-lucky" attitude.

Another example that can be given here is the custom of selling stolen goods to "straights". This seems to be a fairly common practice according to my studies: 42% reported that they had sold to such people. In the informal interviews many said that they had approached people in public parks where they spent a lot of time during the summer. Certain clubs can be used by thieves to sell stolen goods - a sort of "market place bar" in Cavan's (1966) terminology. One interviewee in my sample explained how selling in such places works:

"You know that in some of those clubs there are people who are interested in buying stuff ..."
"Do the guests approach you or ...?"
"No, you walk around and ask ... if there is anyone interested ... And there always is. There are always people interested in buying ... And then, sometimes you get orders and requests to fix something for them, a tape recorder or a camera or something like that ... After that you know who to ask ... after a while you know the people who go there. It's about the same crowd that hangs out there, they'll come to you, sometimes they'll catch you as soon as they see you're there."

Hanging around can also be useful for picking up information about where and when to steal. This is especially important as most thefts do not seem to be planned in the sense of being so a long time in advance of the actual event. Some of the interviewees, especially those who considered themselves as being more or less professional thieves, saw this as a non-professionalism that was frequent mainly among drug addicts.

However, even many of the thieves with no drug problems did not plan their crimes very far in

advance. As reported by McKenna (1972), most crimes
committed by property offenders are not planned more
than a day in advance. A statement by an older,
former thief can serve as an illustration of how
planning can work and how information can be picked
up by hanging around:

"Did you usually plan your thefts?"
"No, not really ... it happened when the money was
nearly gone ... Then we went out to have a sauna
and a good meal during the afternoon instead of
sitting around drinking ..."
"Was there someone who came up with an idea for a
break-in when you sat around?"
"It differs ... sometimes someone showed up and
gave us a tip about where the box safe was at the
pay-office or something ... These people who had
had a job for a week or two and when they got
their salary, stretched their neck to see where
the money was kept."
"But it wasn't anything that you had agreed on
beforehand?"
"No, they just dropped in - they knew we were
sitting there drinking. And then they said - 'try
it', but you never knew whether something would
come out of it. It was always like **gambling.** You
seldom knew anything in advance.

In the insecure and unpredictable world criminals
live in, some of the hangouts such as bars, parks
and pool-halls, can function also as predictable and
stable factors in their lives. One of the petty
thieves I talked to even referred to his bar as
being his family, since he didn't have a
conventional one. The bars criminals frequent thus
often serve the double function of being both
"market place" and "home-territory" bars.
    Places other than the known hangouts could also be
used to meet potential buyers of stolen goods,
friends, etc. (One of them was the waiting room in
the employment exchange office!) One interviewee
reported, for example, how he had taken advantage of

a situation at a local night-club.

> ... Once I was out dancing at Baldakinen, where I
> met this young couple, you see ... They were
> sitting and talking and of course I listened in
> ... They were saying that they hoped to be able to
> buy a color-TV and a stereo ... Well, time passed,
> and when it was almost twelve I went over to them
> and patted the guy on the shoulder and said: "I
> couldn't help hearing you talking. Well, you see
> I'm just out on leave from prison but I have a
> color-TV and a stereo at home that I'm planning to
> sell ... ." Sure enough they came along. I wrote
> them a receipt for the stuff and got the money. So
> that was a nice little transaction!

Interestingly, the ability to take advantage of a
given opportunity is not only seen as instrumental,
but is also reflected in the prestige system of the
thieves' world. Sutherland notes, for example, how
thieves are judged by their "larceny sense", in the
same way as "business sense" is applied to
businessmen.

Mixing of "free time" and "work time"

Some of the quotes above illustrate how what for
most other groups would be considered leisure time
has been converted into work time. The inmates
reported that even strolling down a street and
glancing in windows could lead to contacts for
selling stolen goods or that catching sight of a
brand new color-TV standing outside a television
store could lead to a theft on the spur of the
moment.

As noted by Zerubavel (1979), the social
organization of modern society provides individuals
with private and public time as well as private and
public spheres, which gives people a means of
controlling social accessibility. For people with
ordinary jobs this mainly provides a means to
becoming socially **inaccessible**, to being able to

concentrate at work and to being left in private at home. This ,as I see it, is also something that facilitates an orientation to the present.

For criminals, the private and public spheres are much more undefined. To support themselves they have to become socially accessible, e.g. hanging around bars, cafes, restaurants, etc. Simmel has described sociability as interaction for interaction's own sake, without any other purpose than enjoyment of the moment and without any consequences beyond the encounter itself and hence a de-emphasis of objective purposes and extrinsic rewards.

One can speculate whether this type of undistorted sociability is actually less common among criminals than among other groups, even though it might appear to be the opposite for an outsider. A comparison with the professional gambler is useful in this context:

Another aspect of the gambler's use of the term action arises from the fact that action and the chance-taking it involves may constitute the source of the gambler's daily livelihood. Thus, when he asks **where the action is he is not merely seeking situations of action, but also situations in which he can practice his trade.** (Goffman, 1969:139) (my emphasis)

Fast action and decisions.

The other element in the special kind of future orientation that I have ascribed to the criminal lifestyle concerns certain situations criminals find themselves in. The very nature of illegal enterprises, i.e. their being illegal and thus liable to punishment, often requires fast action. It is thus necessary for criminals to be one step ahead while stealing, conning, robbing, buying drugs, etc. Roebuck in his book *Criminal Typology* describes how robbers are proud of having "nerves" and the ability to quickly evaluate a situation. The con men, on the other hand, were proud of their ability to make a fast judgement of people and to quickly devise a strategy to suit the situation and the particular victim involved.

Making use of the situation

The drug addicts in my studies reported that purchasing drugs was mainly dependent upon two things: access to money and connections. Both have to be available at the same time. In addition, the occasion must be properly used if full advantage is to be achieved. The following two quotations illustrate this relation and how it is related to a future time orientation. This interviewee talked about being a pusher:

> ... if a big load comes in to town it's important to be the first one there and to have a lot of money so you can be there as number one. If I get there a little late, then I'd be number two and that changes the whole situation, it gets more expensive. So as soon as you find out, you have to act ...

A former addict talked about how he used all his available money to buy drugs, and he explained why:

> "... Well, you see, it doesn't matter how much money you have. If I have five hundred crowns or a thousand, I'll spend it all as soon as I get through to the man."
> "So the guys selling drugs are hard to get hold of?"
> "Yeah, when they've got something they're really difficult to get in touch with, so you try to buy all you can. And also, you have to be economical. It's cheaper the more you buy, you have to get hold of all the stuff you can."

In Goffman's (1977) terminology this type of behavior could be described as "insurance behavior", as a coping mechanism. The need for this type of

insurance is connected with the fact that making
effective use of time is much more difficult in the
criminal world, one of the reasons being that time
synchronization is less common than among other
groups. In the more regulated world people keep to
their roles and duties in a more predictable way and
expect that agreed times will be kept. Thus, if you
know with a fair degree of certainty that someone
can be reached at work between 9 a.m. and 5 p.m.,
the need to make fast, vital decisions based on the
availability of a certain person is allayed. You
know that you can always get him at a certain time
and place. The difficulty of getting in touch with
strategic people is one reason for having to make
fast decisions. Another, more obvious one, as noted
above, is the very involvement in criminal
enterprises. For most people there exists some form
of a reserve for the correction of mistakes in
everyday life. This, however is not the case for
criminals at work:

What is special about criminal enterprise ... is
the narrowness of this reserve and hence the high
price that must be paid for thoughtlessness and bad
breaks. (Goffman, 1967:166)

Keeping cool

Goffman describes how people with jobs that require
fast decisions are often proud of their ability to
make them and to "cope". This certainly seems to be
a common trait of most criminals (perhaps with the
possible exception of the forger who can perform his
crimes alone and undisturbed). In general fast
action seems to be highly valued, as well as the
ability to remain in control even in situations that
are unpredictable and dramatic. One of the
interviewees even declared, that he enjoyed being
chased by the police.

Almost 40% of my sample enjoyed the excitement of
stealing. According to the taped interviews, the
reason for this was the pure excitement and also the
control and management of the situation that they

felt during the act of stealing. "You get sort of cool, you see ..." Remaining cool is a necessary "work skill", but, as with most work skills, it becomes something that one is proud of. The concentration on the job on hand and the necessity of being one step ahead in any possible action is clearly illustrated in Goddard's description of one of the experiences of a drug dealer waiting for a man he thinks is going to try to attack him:

> I'm really wound up now, really focused on the moment. Not nervous, but like I'm on a hair trigger, ready to explode at a touch. And I liked it. I like the feeling. (1980:46)

Time synchronization

Sorokin, among others, has emphasized the importance of agreed-upon time and expressed this in the following way:

The possession of means and ways to "time" the behaviour of the members of any group in such a way that each member apprehends "the appointed time" in the same way as do other members has been possibly the most urgent need of social life at any time and at any place. Without this, social life in itself is impossible. (1943:173)

Furthermore, Moore, (1963) has pointed to the importance that temporal ordering has for social order to exist at all. The importance and priorities of different time appointments naturally vary between different cultures and different groups. In every culture some schedules and appointments are considered to be more important than others. The punctual keeping of working-hours is something that is given a high priority in our society.

Criminals, of course, have their own priorities. In contrast to many situations in the criminal world where time is used flexibly, some times are more rigidly fixed. This is the case, for example, when addicts are supposed to pay for their drugs:

> There ain't no room for bull-shitting in that
> world ... It's not like business in the straight
> world where you can get your payments postponed
> and then leave the matter to the collectors and
> let them take it out of your salary or something,
> things like that just don't exist. A thousand
> crowns is a thousand crowns, not nine hundred and
> ninety-eight crowns, you see ... and it's gotta be
> handed over at three o'clock, not at six o'clock
> ... There ain't no half-way points.

The addicts reported that it was important to pay
for drugs on time as they were scared of reprisals
if they broke the agreement. However, even though
those reprisals were sometimes carried out, normally
they were not. For most of the addicts interviewed
the only - but still important - consequence of
their not paying on time was that they were not
trusted in the future as pushers.

Flexibility can, however be equally important. The
elasticity in time that criminals have in their
operations is partly due to the special adjustments
they have to make when dealing with conventional
society and its time schedules. Letkemann has
reported how bank robbers prefer to rob banks on
Mondays, for example, since banks have most money on
that particular day. He also gives an example of how
a certain amount of elasticity is needed in timing
the right occasion:

> While interviewing an urban bank robber I had
> little success in having him respond to the
> question "What time of the day is the best time to
> hit a bank?" He finally responded by saying,"Well,
> you can't tell, you see - you may not be able to
> find a parking spot". He noted that sometimes
> robbers are obliged to cruise around the block
> repeatedly before a suitable parking spot ma-
> terialized. The urban bank robber can neither
> doublepark nor park some distance from the bank.
> The problem of parking, which may be only an
> annoyance to the shopper, is a vital consideration

to the bank robber. (1973:96)

A special present orientation due to regulated time

Max Weber saw the privileged as present oriented since they were able to maintain and expand their present:

Their kingdom is "of this world". They live for the present and by exploiting their great past. The sense of dignity of the negatively privileged strata naturally refers to a future lying beyond the present, whether it is of this life or of another. (1978:934)

While Weber stressed the importance of the past and present situations of privileged groups as a reason for their orientation to the present, I will instead emphasize the planned and ordered future that those groups usually have.

The constant state of preparedness for taking advantage of opportunities in the criminal lifestyle leads to a special kind of orientation to the future. The consequence of this is that most criminals are psychologically less oriented to the present or the "here and now" than groups that lead a more regulated life. An example of the inherent unpredictability of the criminal lifestyle is this statement by a former addict and thief:

... it's like a cycle, you see, where you reach a sort of climax. When you've been in business, you've had a good car and ... then somehow everything blows. You begin by selling your car or trading it in for a less expensive one and some drugs. And then you have to start from scratch again. That's how it works, year after year ...

Most people, through their more stable occupational and family situations, have a rather good idea of their time-schedule and what is going to happen the next day or the next week. Thus people who live a more routine life can afford to be oriented to the present. As long as these routines of everyday life continue without interruption one can concentrate on the here and now of the situation.

In general criminals, and addicts in particular, reported that they had difficulties in keeping appointments when they were "in the life". This increases the feeling of instability and insecurity and creates a sense of anxiety, which is a further argument against the picture of criminals as being happy-go-lucky and present oriented. The anxiety of suddenly remembering that something should have been done or that some appointment should have been kept does not lead to an enjoyment of and a resting in the present. A quote from a former addict can serve as an example:

> "It's hell that you feel so good on drugs, nothing ever gets done ... You freak out ... You meet a girl, well then maybe you've already got something planned but you forget it all and just take off with her for the next nine days to Germany, or whatever."
> "You don't care?"
> "Sure you do because you mean it when you say it but you get very anxious afterwards ... But you just don't think about it at the time."

Life in the streets forbids regulation of time and thereby to a degree reflexion, prison on the other hand consists of regulated time. Thus, Sutherland (1937) has noted that the only time thieves really reflect on their long-term future occurs when they are imprisoned. This was also confirmed in many of the interviews I carried out in prisons. When asked about what type of work they wanted to have in the future, a common answer was:

> Well, I have thought about different things ... you see, here you really get the time and chance to think about those things.

Side-bets

Outside prison criminals often get caught in what Becker (1960) calls "side-bets", which strengthen their criminal commitment. Out of prison, many of those interviewed said they often found themselves stuck in situations they had not really intended to get into but once there, they had to find a way to get out of them. A situation described by a heroin addict who worked as a forger can serve as an illustration:

> Last time I escaped from prison I was living in Lund at a place where a lot of bums live, criminals and so on. I needed bank accounts and stuff like that, ID-cards and ...While they were trying to get those things I got drugs in advance, you see ... But they couldn't get the stuff so I had to go out and steal myself, you see. So I stole a stereo in Malmö, took a cab to Lund which they paid for and then I got drugs since they knew I had the stereo in Malmö, then back to Malmö in a cab to get the stereo, back to Lund again in a cab. It's really complicated.

Although rather complicated, this serves as an example of how constant lines of commitments can be caused by side-bets - previous promises and actions which have been agreed upon. It also gives an example of how a future orientation is involved in a situation that might appear as oriented to the present.

Perhaps this reason, together with the described need for always being alert and prepared, is why the interviewed thieves so often said that it was the most tiresome job you could have.

Coping

Though Goffman uses the concept of coping in those cases where an individual "makes realistic efforts to minimize the eventfulness - the fatefulness - of his moments ..." (1969:128), I think the concept can be applied to many criminals. The way they cope, however, is naturally different from what Goffman refers to as the Calvinistic solution to life, where the individual divides his day's activities so that each has a small contributive consequence.[3]

Nelkin has used Goffman's differentiation between coping as one adaption and defence as another. She descibes poor seasonal workers who earn their living picking fruit and vegetables and live an uncertain and unplanned life because of the unpredictability of the weather and harvest times. According to her, the seasonal workers adopt a defensive behavior, that is, they relinquish all possibilities of control and, instead, seek some form of relief:

Time is often killed by waiting and anticipation. One waits for the end of the workday, payday, the next crop, or the trip home ... Tomorrow is vaguely anticipated to be better than today ... Yet there is no planning or activity directed toward realizing these expectations ... In sum, the migrant's sense of the relation between effort and return, between behavior and its consequences, is based on the assumption that their environment may be neither predicted nor controlled. In this context, time is present-oriented, irrational and highly personal ... (1970:37-38)

Kurt Lewin, writing about the unemployed, reflected on the apathy that distinguishes this group, which is so commonly associated with being out of work:

An analysis of this behavior shows the importance of that psychological factor which commonly is called "hope". Only when the person gives up hope does he stop **"actively reaching out"**. He loses his energy, he ceases the planning, and finally, he even stops wishing for a better future ... (1948:103)(my emphasis)

Underprivileged people in general as Schwartz (1975) has pointed out have a higher tolerance for waiting, because even if they have something else they **can** do, they might not have anything **better** to do.

In many people's minds, groups such as the above and criminals are associated. I think however that it is important not to mix them together since criminals often see themselves as "men of action". Criminals, as opposed to the groups described above, for example, often use time to "actively reach out", as Lewin put it.

The value of independence

I have tried to explain how the planning or future orientation functions as a work requirement for those leading a criminal lifestyle. In addition criminals often set a great value on personal independence and the ability to make their own time.

In their book *The Delinquent Way of Life*, West and Farrington have given a list of criminologists' views of the values and motivation factors of criminals. The value of independence, however, is not mentioned, which is curious since this struck me as one of the most outstanding features in their value patterns.

As has been noted here, criminals have to adjust to the rest of the society's time when they are carrying out some of their enterprises. There are, however, other occasions when they take a certain pride in not caring for the conventions of time use which conventional society defines as proper behavior. Many of the interviewees stated, for example, how they could not stand waiting in queues when it was not necessary, which often led to them steal things in stores even if they had not intended to at first, thereby hopefully passing the queue.

A craving for independence is naturally related to individualism, as noted by Lukes. This is often mirrored in the reasons for not wanting to become an ordinary "John":

... you see, I don't want to be an ordinary John, it just doesn't work out, you have to have some fun ... I think that we too should have some of the good things in life ... I like to travel for example, so **whenever** it suits me I go to Spain for a couple of weeks. **When, wherever** and **whatever** way that fits my plans and mood. You see, I can get that idea on a Friday night and then on Monday I'll be on the plane ...

As a final example of the importance attached to the highly valued independence factor, this former thief had remained a bachelor in order to keep control of his own time.

"I still have this need for independence. For example, I've had a lot of chances in my day to get married but I've still got that idea in my head, that if I take my coat and my hat - then she says "where are you going?" She doesn't mean anything with it, but it's natural that you ask a question like that if you're living together "where are you going?" And I don't like that because I want to be able to come and go exactly as I want without having someone asking about it ... And I've always been like that."
"Are many thieves like that?"
"**Most** of them ... for example, there was this guy who I was with a lot, that told his wife that he was just going out to buy some rolls and some cream for the coffee. It took eight months before he came back! (laughter). On his way to the store he bumped into some friends and had some drinks with those guys and afterwards they went out breaking (stealing) and got busted the same night."
"Didn't he write or call his wife during that time?"
"No, not once. After those eight months he returned, bought his rolls, came home and she said - those were long rolls (appreciative laughter). That's the plain truth! He was the same, he wanted to come and go as he liked ... Most of them want to be independent and if they are going to, they have to steal."

This highly individualistic attitude can be seen as enabling one to have an orientation to the immediate future. Criminals are less often tied to a family than the rest of the population, even if many of them say that they wish they had a family. Family bonds, however, often imply planning in terms of long-run goals, since it means adjusting to the plans and schedules of several individuals. Most criminals are free from these constraints, arising from mutual considerations, and thus are able to change plans suddenly and take advantage of different opportunities that arise - a necessity if one is to support oneself by crime.

7
SOCIAL SKILLS

It is interesting to note that criminals are said
to be "undersocialized" or "sociopathic", even
though one or more phases of their criminal action
can well involve not only a slavish concern for
what others would expect them to be if they are to
go unnoticed, but also the staking of a great deal
on their being correct in their appraisals.
(Goffman, 1971:277)

Contrary to common beliefs, it will be argued here
that criminals possess social skills in many areas.
The skills that will be discussed concern those of
identifying others, "passing", making contacts, and
managing other people. Due to their peculiar work
situation, their marginal position, and their lack
of formal merits, criminals need and develop the
skills referred to above.
Two main problems within the sphere of social
interactions concerning personal information
confront criminals. One is that of hiding one's own
identity - which is discussed as "appearing normal"
and "passing". The other is that of identifying
others. For criminals, these are vital issues.
Although these social skills are usually
associated with con men, other criminals both need
and possess them as well. Letkemann, who has studied

robbers and safecrackers, writes:

The criminal must take on the role of the "other" in order to take advantage of the civilian. Although it is apparent that such role-taking is necessary for the successful confidence game, its importance in other types of crime is not recognized in related academic literature. (1973:128)

The American sociologist Waldorf gives for example, the following account of different social skills involved in hustling activities:

Regular hustling seems to foster the development of a specific sensitivity. The hustler learns in a short time how to size up people and situations precisely and quickly - to recognize persons who are vulnerable to theft ... how with a team of two one can distract a store clerk at one end of the store while the second robs the other end ... But these are only the mechanics of the hustle; more subtle are the abilities to recognize undercover police and to assess the vulnerability of an individual or a situation ... The skilled street prostitute knows exactly whom to encourage or discourage, whom to avoid at all cost. (1973:13)

The author summarizes nicely some different themes that will be discussed later here, such as the importance of sizing up people, learning whom to trust, appearing normal under stress situations and recognizing important others.

I do not want to argue, of course, that all criminals possess these skills. Naturally, they are more or less skilled and educated in these matters. The analysis below should therefore be seen as something close to an ideal typical account of how they act at times and how they think one should act.

Identifying of others

The concept of identifying has several connotations. The sociologist Stone (1959) points out the difference between identifying **with** someone and identification **of** someone. He argues that Mead's "role-taking" means identification with, but before one is able to do this one has to "place" this someone.[1] In doing this we are helped by outward appearances, gestures, language, etc. Below, I will discuss this identifying of others - who is a crook, an undercover policeman, a presumptive customer, etc.

Identifying other criminals

On several occasions the interviewees mentioned that they were able to "see" whether someone was a crook or not. When I asked **how** they were able to do this, the answers, however, often had a touch of the undefinable - "It's just a feeling,""It's a look in the eyes,""It's not necessarily talking, I think it has more to do with vibrations." As Zerubavel (1982) has pointed out, information about others is often something we see as self-evident, and since we take it for granted, it is difficult to say what we are looking for.

The ability to recognize each other has been mentioned in several autobiographies. In *My Life in Crime* the thief describes one time when he was in Reno, where his ability to "see" the absence of crooks led him to abstain from crime there:

> I also saw that there's no stealing allowed in the town. Everything was in the open, very seldom did they ever have any robbery or burglary. I just **see** it - I don't run into any characters, anybody on the make **or** anything in the saloons and places like that. If there's nine or ten men at a bar and there's two or three thieves there, before the evening's over the three thieves'll be together. I didn't meet anybody at all in Reno. (Martin, 1952:47)

And Waldorf makes the following remark about the addicts he studied:

Dope fiends claim that they can spot another dope fiend with only the most supeficial contact, in many instances without having talked to the other person.

Both physical addiction and the attitudes of the
dope fiend are said to be apparent in gestures and
stance - "in the way he holds himself". (1973:21)

This does not seem to be exclusively for the
trained criminal. In a study of juvenile
delinquents, it is noted that those who have run
away from home have no difficulty in finding equals
in new places by hanging out at the "right places"
where "the actions is".[2]

This is in line with Goffman's (1969) notion that
the traditional mechanisms of acquaintanceship and
personal invitation are not necessary for action-
seekers since the risks of participation serve as
invitation and attraction. Action-seekers seem to
group into a free-masonry where strangers can form a
temporary coalition against the society of
respectables. The action-seekers, as Goffman describes them, could easily find each other in a new
town. One looks for the "right vibrations" or that
"crook-look in the eyes", as some said when feeling
out whether the stranger one talks to at a bar, for
example, is the right kind.

Identifying the police

Criminals also develop a skill for recognizing
undercover police. Here, a "modern thief" who states
that he has so much experience with the police that
he can spot them by looking at them and "feeling
them out":

> You know, there are young policemen with beards
> and long hair drivin' around in old cars with wine
> bottles in their hands. But, you know, I've dealt
> so much with the police that I know them, they
> can't fool me ... you can tell by looking at them
> and you feel it as well ...

This knowledge can and often needs to be
communicated by rather subtle means. Goffman argues
that individuals use "staging clues" to communicate
whether the coast is clear or that there are people

nearby for whom one should keep up one's guard:

In the criminal world, in fact, the warnings that "legit" ears are listening or legit eyes are watching is so important that it has a special name, called "giving office". (1959:183)

Identifying customers and others

Judging character is obviously also necessary if one is selling to "civilians", i.e., not to professional fences, that one does not know. An account of how a thief established contact with a man:

> I was on my way out of Folkets Park, and walked into him and I had a tape-recorder on me and a stereo in the car, so I asked him if he didn't want to buy, it was Christmas, you know, some Christmas presents for his kids, I needed some money. Yeah, sure, he looked at them and we got to know each other.

The thief had earlier talked about how younger people were "freer" and therefore easier to approach. He described this man however, as middle-aged and very properly dressed. Therefore, I asked how he dared to approach him.

> He had something of a crooked look in his face ... a look in his eyes ...

This recognition of people is necessary for criminals if they are to meet new accomplices, sell to new customers or avoid the police. The importance of other people for one's own safety can even lead to a development of memory skills:

> He had only met my friend once ... Suddenly he looked down into his lager and said very quietly: "Your mate is over at the entrance at the right." I looked across and had difficulty in spotting him among the crush of people at the door. Henry smiled when I remarked that he must have an

incredible memory for faces. "It's essential in my business - it can stop you getting into lots of bother." (Crookstone, 1967:10-11)

In prison, a sense of others' reactions is important, on occasions even vital. A quote from an interview from an American study:

There's a thing you develop in prison that's like a radar antenna - a third eye - for danger. You see danger signs all the time, and if you can apply them to yourself, immediately you become in touch with what's going on around you. And especially in prison, you know who dangerous people are, what dangerous situations are, dangerous bulls, dangerous convicts ... (Bull 1972:73)

Identifying in general

Table 25.   "I can easily tell what social level a person belongs to after meeting him only once."

%	Agree	Disagree	No opinion	Sum	N
Inmates	50	26	24	100	(127)
SIFO	29	41	30	100	(125)

For inmates it thus seems less problematic to classify people according to class. A young thief sees this talent, for example, as totally self-evident:

"Is it easier for you as a criminal to classify people?"
"No, anyone can do that. You can tell by clothing and way of talking and how people carry themselves and so on."

I have found quite a different way of thinking in qualitative interviews with non-criminal people. It seems as if the norms in today's society are such that people believe that the social class of an individual **cannot** be identified just like that. Maybe this is due to Sweden's being such a homogeneous society and, due to its ideological background, striving for equality between different social groups.

Identifying and utilizing the special conditions of any given situation

In some situations, such as being caught in the act, criminals need to "act normal" or to "pass". Goffman has noted that the ability to think quickly and act as if everything is normal, is often seen as a gift but is something some groups - such as criminals - get a lot of practice in doing, since they encounter a lot of "strategic moments":

Here, then, is a standard for measuring presence of mind , one involving the ability to come up quickly with the kind of accountings that allow a disturbing event to be assimilated to the normal ... Thieves, of course, have a special need to construct false, good accounts at strategic moments and have a word, "con", to cover ability in this sort of covering. (1972:263)

In the article *Big City Thieves*, the journalist Bowers tells us the following story, which nicely illustrates what was said above:

Recently a woman coming in her West Side apartment house held the front door open for a young man going out with a TV set that looked familiar and pillow-case full of clothing. He smiled, thanked her, and caught a cab. He had just burglarized her apartment. (1967:54)

We are also told that he walked out with "a confident air". Some of the interviewees in my study told me about occasions when they had burglarized an apartment for a TV set or something else, and left the place in a cab like the thief in the quote above. The need to "act normal" during the drive is obvious.

Appearing normal can of course be achieved through different techniques. A few examples: West (1974) points out that thieves play upon the trust in others that pervades in our society and that they use "normal activities", such as "moving furniture", when stealing, in this respect. How one carries oneself and plays the part that one impersonates is obviously important. An illustration of using acting talents is this safe-cracker's ability to "act natural" when a nurse enters the room where he was in the act of opening the hospital's safe:

> She asked me if I was the maintenance man and I said yes, I was. She asked me to come up and fix something. I said I would as soon as I took the box out. I often wondered what she thought the next morning when they found out that the drug room had been robbed. I'll make a bet that she never told anyone that she had seen me the night before. (Chambliss and King, 1972:39)

Even props can be important. Jackson (1972) writes about a dope runner who walked around with a horn which he never blew, but used as a front when he hitchhiked late at night. Letkemann (1973), who refers to "the misuse of social convention" by criminals, describes a safe-cracker who used to dress like a businessman and walk around with a briefcase because that gave him the look of respectability which gave him the "key to practically any place".

As was seen by the above, the type of impression that criminals want - or try - to make on other people is often the reverse of that which non-criminal people want to make. As Goffman (1959) has pointed out, legitimate performance sometimes stresses the unique in a situation, while false performance (often needed by a criminal) emphasizes the routineness is a situation, in order to draw attention **away** from himself and allay suspicion. On the legitimate side, one can take, for example, the circus ring master who has to give every show a shimmer of uniqueness, "And **now**, ladies and gentlemen, this is the one and only ...", several times every night. Guides and tour-leaders are other examples of professionals who have to emphasize the uniqueness in their performance, in order to convey an enthusiasm for the shown object, the sight-seeing spot, to constantly new audiences.

Normal appearances for others

In order to know that others are what they claim to be, or in order to fit in during illegal activities as described above, criminals need a knowledge of what is typical for other groups. "Passing"[3] is also used by criminals to fit in, to hide one's identity,[4] in more ordinary circumstances:

> When I get out I dress right and no one can tell that I've been here (in prison), not a soul, and they absolutely won't be able to find out what kind of business I'm in. (laughter)

However, using one's knowledge about others is perhaps most vital when it comes to committing crime. Goffman uses the terms "predator" and "prey" to describe different roles. His analysis of the "predators'" (here criminals) concerned with normal appearances is helpful in the present context. He points out that they need to become "phenomenologists, close students of everyday life, not, of course, their own but what the subject takes to be of everyday life". (1972:260) Letkemann's report about a prospective bank-robber is illustrative:

> Number 41 stated that he once entered a bank to rob it, and noticed a man standing behind the bank counter with a foot on a chair and his arms folded. He knew this man was a policeman, so he left the bank ... he went on to explain that a

bank manager may sit on a table with his feet
hanging down, or sit on a chair and have his feet
on a desk, but "he will never stand with one foot
on a chair!" (1973:149)

One advantage (in addition to the obvious one) in
stealing from wealthy people accoring to Martin is
the following, also an example of thieves' knowledge
of group behavior:

The only place you can do that (walking right in)
is your wealthy communities. Your wealthy people
don't holler over the back porch and say, Hello,
Mrs Smith, will you keep an eye on the house while
I'm gone? Your wealthy people don't holler over
back fences. (1952:93)

This knowledge of what others consider normal is
essential even in periferal things. That parking is
a problem in bank robbery is something that is not
often considered. Knowledge of typical group behavior can be valuable even here, as is seen from
the following:

"Suppose you can't find a parking lot?"
"Oh, we double-park. You see, in these small
towns, especially country towns, we drive a pick-
up truck; if people see a truck double-parked,
motor running, they think it's a farmer who's gone
into the bank for a minute - so it takes away all
suspicion. We make sure it's an old truck, but
with a fairly good motor in it." (Letkemann,
1973:97)

The thieves I interviewed claimed they could easily
find hidden money in people's homes. This puzzled
me, but Letkemann's explanation, of "social behavior
knowledge", makes it more obvious:

A home does not have a cash register, nor,
necessarily, a safe. Therefore burglar must make
quick interpretations as to the most probable

location of the cash. The mental activity here is really a game of wits - of operating on the basis of **reciprocal expectations.** He proceeds on the **assumption he has regarding routine family behavior,** he anticipates uniformity in architecture as well as in styles of placing valuables. (Ibid.:55)(my emphasis)

Skills in making contact

Perhaps it is the knowledge about others that enables criminals to make contact with strangers comparatively easily.

Table 26.   "It's easy for me to make contact with strangers."

%	Agree	Disagree	No opinion	Sum	N
Traditional thieves	79	8	13	100	(38)
All inmates	65	11	24	100	(133)
Control group	63	10	27	100	(198)

One can thus conclude that inmates do not have greater difficulty than the control group in making contact with strangers. Traditional thieves even seem to view it as easier. I think this is of importance, since problems of sociability are often emphasized in the picture of criminals. I do not want to imply that criminals should be especially skilled in long-term relationships - they probably have problems in that area. But many have a good ability to strike up a conversation, relate to strangers, etc.

I was impressed by the inmates' openness and their narrative talents as compared to other groups I have interviewed regarding pretty much the same areas: their lives, work, interests, etc. West and Farrington obviously got the same picture; they write about "the typical, extroverted, gregarious recidivist" (1977:15). Maybe these narrative talents, the talkativeness, etc. can be explained by the fact that these groups have a lot of free time in the streets, in prison, etc. to develop and get feed-back for such skills.

Managing people

Another social skill that criminals tend to develop is that of managing people. I will try to illustrate how this can be done as well as the reasons and needs behind it.

That criminals rely heavily on social skills in general probably depends on their lack of formal merits to fall back on. As Shibutani has noted:

... any person who must depend upon the cooperation of others becomes responsive to their views. He must be careful to conduct himself in a manner designed not to alienate them. He cannot afford to do anything that would lead others to hesitate, withdraw their support, or oppose his efforts. (1961:90)

Warner et al., in the article *The Hero, the Sambo and the Operator*, discuss the characterization of subordinated groups, such as minorities, the poor, and women. Previously in the literature, two conceptions dominated, the "hero" and the "sambo". In the first model, the hero is portrayed as rebellious; coupled with this is the idea that oppression produces an ennoblement of character. The sambo, on the other hand, represent a picture of the oppressed as deferential, apathetic, passive, etc. He enjoys, rather than resists, his treatment and identifies with the values of his oppressors. Blacks who use hair straighteners and Tory workers in Britain are used as examples. Sambos are said to internalize a maladaptive set of values which makes it impossible for them to respond intelligently to available opportunities.

The authors argue that for subordinate groups, a third alternative is more prevalent, namely the social type "operators". By this, the authors mean a type of behavior consciously calculated and adopted to take advantage of a situation. An operator can, for example, take advantage of the situation by pretending to be and taking the role of a sambo. An example is found in school girls who deliberately hide their academic competence in order to attract the opposite sex.[5]

The operator model offers an appreciation of the manoeuvres of the oppressed and the dramaturgical skills involved.[6] Some of the skills, as the authors see it, are sensitivity in ferreting out between-the-lines meanings, showing deference, and seeming "incompetent" or stupid. All these are seen as manipulative strategies. Even though examples have already been given of these techniques in the present work, I will elaborate on this theme a bit more.

Using deference for example is a means that can help young delinquents in their encounters with the police.[7] Showing respect and be seen as "serious and responsible" can help criminals in their dealings with probation officers and courts. Addicts sometimes use their addiction to argue that they were forced to steal or to sell drugs.

Thieves, however, tend to sneer at this last device, calling it manipulative. Since thieves themselves are not morally against manipulating people in some circumstances, the reason for this might be that they see through the addicts' act and get upset because the authorities are taken in. This moral self-righteousness on the part of the thieves is based on indignation (tinged perhaps with a little chagrin) that a class of people that they look down upon can get away with such things. Furthermore, if the actual drug addiction is made a reason for lenient treatment, the (non-addicted) thieves are at a disadvantage. This indignation is clearly shown in a quotation from nine "lifers" who wrote an open letter to a Swedish newspaper because they were upset about how a well-known big drug dealer had told the police about drug dealing in prison:

As far as the drug situation is concerned, you're lying a blue streak! You're trying to cash in on the journalistic myth about the prisons swimming in dope. Where does this myth about the surplus of narcotics in prison come from? We'll tell you - it comes from the buddies who get caught committing a crime while on "pass" or just after being released, who tell the court that "they were forced to commit a crime to pay off the drug debt they had incurred in jail." Just like the ones who claim they got hooked while in the pen. Nonsense!! But they tell this to the courts to raise sympathy and understanding, so they'll get a lighter sentence - just like you did! (Expressen Aug. 25, 1982:7)

Addicts are supposedly more likely to take social welfare assistance. A man who had been a thief as well as an addict related how his changing status implied changes in his outlook towards such help and how he became skillful in manipulating social welfare assistants:

"You didn't go and get on welfare when you could steal, that went against our 'code of ethics' ... But then when you started takin' heroin and morphine and stuff, you weren't so good a thief. It's true that the more dope you take, the worse a thief you become ... Then of course it was good to be on social welfare and you learned how to manipulate them. For years on and off, I went to the social welfare office flying high on shit, but they never noticed a thing - they always thought I was sick when I came. But if I wasn't turned on, I didn't bother going at all - too big a hassle."
"What did you tell them?"
"That I wanted to get into Hindby (a treatment center for addicts) and quit, or get a job. You always found excuses, like if you said you were going to an introduction meeting at Hindby, the next time you came you said the they didn't answer when you called ... Then the social worker said,

'Yeah, I don't believe it.' But they swallowed it anyhow. It's true that they'll believe you if you're a good actor."

An "idealization in performances"[8] is sometimes used to achieve goals. West relates how conventional societal beliefs about when an offender should be pitied can be used:

The thief has usually acquired some practical legal sense of how to best present his case (e.g. getting a regular job, or bringing a tearful mother, or pregnant fiancee to court).(1974:203)

Enhancing one's opponent is another trick that can be used. In Bull's study of former criminals this account, from an interview, of how counselors can be manipulated is given:

If making a counselor feel or think - or a therapist - making him feel or think that he's an exception will benefit you, then you do what you have to do to make him feel or think that he is an exception. But he's still the enemy. And you never forget that that ball-point pen is his weapon. So you try to say and do what will impress him favorably with the least fuss and bother. (1972:70)

Reasons for social skills

One reason - the lack of formal merits - that criminals acquire social skills has been mentioned above. In the following section, I will give a few more instances of how they need and learn those skills: through their work situation, their prison experiences, and their marginal situation.

Work

In many occupations the need for social skills and managing people is obvious, such as in service-related branches. Thieves in particular among criminals have reasons for developing such skills. One explanation for why traditional thieves to a

higher degree than the control group state that they
easily make contact with strangers might be their
work situation. For example, they must sometimes
approach strangers when selling stolen goods. Miller
describes a bar whose patrons were partly
criminals.[9] The thieves there had an intermediate
position and had to mix with several groups of
people:

Unlike the businessman and hip squares, however,
thieves are not segregated from the other
participants all of the time. To the contrary, the
significance of the thieves in the setting derives
from their activities as intermediaries between the
various patron groups and between deviant and non-
deviant activities. They offer their services to
other criminals when those services are requested,
and also they are prepared to offer goods and
services to non-deviant patrons who may approach
them. (1978:210)

Another reason that thieves acquire social skills
is their business orientation (coupled with their
marginal and stigmatized position). This makes them
aware of and concerned about the impression they
make:

... where there is the possibility of alternative
responses, as in the case of a client who might
accept, decline, delay, become insulted, or laugh
upon being asked to conclude a transaction, there is
much concern over the kind of impression that is
being made. (Shibutani, 1961:90)

Trust

Trust is essential both in determining who of the
others is reliable, and in establishing a reputation
of being trustworthy oneself. Social skills are
evident in the first aspect, that of judging others,
but they are also important in the second aspect.
Art Pepper relates, for example, an incident where
the police out of revenge tried to make him look
like someone who had "ratted" just because he would
not. Social skills of a high order were necessary

for him to regain the respect of other inmates. It was certainly not enough just to state his innocence.

Different situations require varying degrees of "character reading" when deciding whether or not to trust someone. Goode notes situations where people do not know each other and are not supposed to question each other, as was supposedly common for the American frontier towns. These norms closely resemble those of the criminal world:

Of course, in such a situation almost everyone develops competence in "reading" the symbols, gestures, modes of speech, and so forth, in short, the cues by which people ascertain to which extent the claims are justified. (1978:255)

He expands this reasoning by saying that even if people in such circumstances feel more free to make exaggerated claims about themselves, others are less constrained to believe them. Goode's analysis of these aspects of the frontier town is comparable to the criminal life. The inmates I interviewed expressed great moral indignation towards those who thought they were "something special", or made, as they saw it, unjustified claims. This is, of course, quite natural, as believing these claims could lead them into undesirable situations: e.g. trusting someone who claims he is good at break-ins, but who fouls up while making one. Therefore an emphasis is make on ferreting out phony talk or behavior. Irwin says:

To be all right, you mustn't be a phony. A phony is a person who puts up bogus fronts. Criminals are not against fronts. They are well aware of and skilled at front management. They admire persons who maintain good fronts, but they object to phony fronts. Putting up a phony front is making claims about yourself which aren't true for purposes other than humor or stealing, promising something at the moment for the sake of impression and not coming through later, or pretending to believe one thing and then by actions or words revealing that you actually believe something else. (1972:124)

Since contacts and trustworthy relationships are so important for criminals, it is not surprising that they more than others react strongly to a "bogus front" which to someone else might even be slightly amusing.

When we talked about possible social skills among criminals, the respondents in my study emphasized that they were more able to determine whom to trust and mistrust than most people. This is also reflected in the answers to the statement below from the questionnaire.

Table 27.   "One cannot be too careful in one's dealings with other people."

%	Agree	Disagree	No opinion	Sum	N
All inmates	58	9	32	100	(127)
SIFO	28	32	40	100	(125)

Determining reliability in one's accomplices may be even more important today, since criminals are said to work with different associates from time to time more often than before. Several scholars have argued that professional criminals do not base their criminal projects on strong, long-time relationships but on the different requirements for personnel in skills, numbers, etc. for carrying out the crime.[10]

What this interviewee says about finding and pairing up with associates is illustrative, and it is also contrary to a situation where everybody knows each other in the criminal world:

... you always bump into another crook somehow ... There's always something that clicks between ya'. It doesn't have to be much, just a little. Everything doesn't have to be compatible because this ain't forever. It ain't like having a family or something, 'cause then it gotta fit one hundred percent. It ain't like that when you commit a crime, it's just temporary - you need someone for a short while.

Marginalism

In this study it has been argued that one possible reason for a criminal's individualism and claim of responsibility is that he can be viewed as a marginal man. Since it is important in the present context as well, I will give some further evidence below to support the argument.

A high percentage, 65%, of all inmates seem to belive that it is easy for them to associate with different types of people.

Table 28. "Do you think that criminals, due to their way of living, have an easier time socializing with different kinds of people than ordinary people have?"

	%	N
Yes	65	(68)
No	35	(36)
Sum	100	(104)

Table 29. "If Yes, why?"

	%	N
Because you have to learn whom to trust and whom to distrust.	49	(36)
Because in terms of stealing and selling goods you must be able to size people up.	27	(20)
Because you meet so many more people as a criminal than ordinary people do.	62	(46)
Because you have to be able to handle officials and others in order not to get caught.	27	(20)

Note: 30 % of those who answered the preceeding question did not answer this question.

The most common reason why criminals consider it easy to socialize with different types of people is that they associate with so many different groups. This was also confirmed in a question as to what type of people they usually associated with outside prison. Only about a third of the inmates met mainly with their respective groups, i.e. thieves with thieves and addicts with addicts. Around a fifth remained mainly with their family and almost half of the traditional thieves stated that they associated mainly with "ordinary people" while on the outside. Given that this information is correct, criminals should be helped in their development of adjustment skills since they encounter different cultures.

The socializing with ordinary people as well as with criminals seems to be a matter of preference for many. This is evident from the tables below:

Table 30.   "I feel more at home among addicts than among ordinary people."

%	Agree	Disagree	No opinion	Sum	N
Traditional thieves	8	87	5	100	(37)
Modern thieves	29	43	29	100	(42)
Mixed	58	32	11	100	(19)
Addicts	33	44	22	100	(18)

Table 31.   "I feel more at home among thieves than among ordinary people."

%	Agree	Disagree	No opinion	Sum	N
Traditional thieves	20	57	23	100	(35)
Modern thieves	31	41	29	100	(42)
Mixed	45	44	11	100	(18)
Addicts	17	61	22	100	(18)

Table 32.   "I feel more at home among ordinary
             people than among thieves or addicts."

%	Agree	Disagree	No opinion	Sum	N
Traditional thieves	39	36	25	100	(36)
Modern thieves	22	44	34	100	(32)
Mixed	26	49	26	100	(19)
Addicts	22	50	28	100	(18)

Gale Miller's (1978) reflection on cohesiveness in deviant groups might be helpful in explaining why more of those interviewed did not prefer their own group. He argues that deviant groups consist of informal segments rather than wider occupational groups. Although the members of each segment might be committed to each other, the rivalry between them, the lack of general loyalty due to the primary interest of making money (or attaining drugs), and the concern of the immediate social niches and not of the general common position in society limits the general group consciousness and commitment.

Not only is belonging and identity complicated at a general level; there are also differences between groups. The results reflect, I think, my impression of the traditional thieves as being more like ordinary people than addicts in their value pattern, and as having an instrumental approach to their crimes as a means of support rather than an emotional or ideological one like addicts. To a question about who among other criminals is most respected and appreciated outside prison, the most common answer in the traditional thief group was "the ones who live like the squares, but support themselves illegally". Of the traditional thieves, 45% agreed to this, as opposed to only 14% of the addicts. More among the traditional thieves also stated that they had lived as square-johns themselves:

Table 33.   "Have you lived a square type of life?"

%	Yes	No	Sum	N
Traditional thieves	70	30	100	(37)
Modern thieves	65	35	100	(46)
Mixed	53	47	100	(19)
Addicts	50	50	100	(18)

Especially the older thieves stated that they preferred seeing non-criminals when they were out of prison: "It's like you need to get away from work, you know, and that type of jargon ... ", "If you don't change to other types of people, you'll get really dumb. You need to speak about other things than we do here ...", "I don't like people with problems, it's damn tiring. So I see relatives or other friends when I'm on the outside."

Even the respondents who did not prefer the company of others than criminals had tried at times to go straight. Usually this implied working with non-criminals and maybe also having a relationship with a non-criminal woman, meeting her family and friends, etc.

In *The Time Game* there is a description about how a former convict and addict successfully makes it in the conventional world, and then only a few years before graduation from university, leaves his work, gets a divorce, drops out of university and returns to drugs. Empey comments in the postscript that the convict is a marginal man and that this explains some of his problems. Dunn, the convict, says himself:

When I was a kid I had a difficult time switching from being a "hard guy" in the street gang to a cool professional. It was the second most difficult change I have ever tried to make. The most difficult change was the last one. It was even harder to play the middle-class role. I have never experienced a complete sense of belonging anywhere. (Manocchio and Dunn, 1970:259)

Similar experiences, in a less dramatic form, are quite general for most criminals. As several authors have pointed out, being marginal often includes increased self-awareness and demands on the self, as well a distanced view of oneself and the world. Dunn talks, for example, about "playing the middle-class role". Middle-class people probably see themselves as "middle-class", but hardly "playing" the middle-class role. He also mentioned switching from the "hard guy" to "the cool professional" - which is stepping outside oneself and viewing both oneself and others and their roles in quite a detached manner.

Prison experiences

It is usually believed that prison destroys social abilities.[11] This is of course true for many. But at the same time it can be seen as a social training ground for getting along with others: different inmates with different personalities, staff of various kinds, etc. An old safe-cracker spoke for example about difficulties in changing his style of talking when he got out, but also of the skills in adjustment that he learned in prison:

"When you walk out of this joint, you have to turn your talking around."
"Isn't that difficult?"
"Yeah, sure, it's damn difficult, but I think those in here have a real good adjustment ability ... ability to adjust to different situations. You gotta have it if you're gonna make it, otherwise you'll break down. Most in here can deal with all kinds of environments, you'll learn that in here, 'cause otherwise you won't make it."

Proudness and enjoyment from social skills

As with any other skill, social skills are something one can be proud of and also something one can enjoy. Cheating others about one's own identity or intents can, for example, be appreciated.

> A thief thinks square-johns are crazy ... When I was stealing, why I lived a lie. You automatically - what's the word - acclimate yourself to it and you just go ahead and live it. I mean, you enjoy it and get some guy in the bar and you're sittin' there and you lay an awful story on the guy and he's sittin' there shaking his head like a nut on the end of a string you know, and he's buying the story. You get up and go home and you say, "Why, I had an enjoyable evening." (Chambliss and King, 1972:76-77)

In Jackson's *In the Life*, the interviewee who states that he has done every criminal activity except false checks, murder and rape, says he prefers using stolen credit cards:

> With the cards you got to play the part, and as far as playing the part goes I'm a pretty fair actor. You pull up and put some story on a young kid and he's going to go for it real quick. (1972:129)

The social skills can, of course, be used after one has left the criminal life, and especially when working with criminals. A former addict, who presently works in a treatment home for addicts, states that he has good use of his social skills in detecting manipulative attempts from those he tries to rehabilitate:

> You notice from the guys how skillfull you yourself were once when they try to pull the same stuff on you - I really have to try hard not to laugh, 'cause I know exactly when they're tryin' something, and then they say, "Damn, how dumb I was to try - you've been around so long ..." But if they go into the social welfare office and there's a sweet young thing from the school of

social work sitting there, it's all over in two
seconds flat. Even with a guy - it's as easy as
anything.

8
THE PHILOSOPHY OF MONEY

Money, or rather the attainment of money, is often given as the reason why someone gets involved in property crimes. As early as 1937, Sutherland remarked in his classic study *The Professional Thief:*

> When thieves finish the day's work, they generally congregate in hangouts. There they are thieves together regardless of their rackets, with one common love - money - and one common enemy - the law. (1937:158)

Shover (1971) gives a similar description of burglars as interested in money as a "motor" for their particular lifestyle. He also points out that in order to even be considered a thief, a man must be "kinky", i.e., have an eye for opportunities to make money.

Even juvenile delinquents, who are often assumed to be less rational in their crimes, according to West and Farrington (1977), give material gain as an explanation for their illegal acts.

Different meanings attached to money

The significance of money, for criminals, is

somewhat different than for most people in the conventional world. The former emphasized that they did not want money to assume a principal place in their lives, while at the same time they were not prepared to live a life of penury.

Sellerberg (1978), made a study of consumers; in this study a high value was placed on being a "smarty". For the consumer, this meant being able to buy at special rates, or finding cheap things in a number of ways. They liked the challenge of getting as much for one's money as possible. Being a smarty obviously means different things for different groups: for criminals, it implied handling one's business in a clever way. Many thieves would find it demeaning to bargain about a price. An elderly thief is proud of having restored his apartment and some old furniture himself, but denies being economical:

No, I'm not. If I want something I'll buy it whatever it costs. I don't ask the price ... I don't think I've ever asked first, "How much is this?"

In the interviews the inmates themselves claimed a difference between them and ordinary people. They said that the squares can not handle "big money": some of them could not even win a jackpot without getting nervous.

This is probably true to a certain extent. For most, drastic financial changes would create an anomic situation in their lives. While making a study of ordinary people, I was told by someone that he participated in the state lottery every month. Since the study included questions about finances and consumption, I asked him how he would spend his money if he won. He began talking about this, and then after a while he said, "Actually, I think about it at night sometimes, and it would be a nightmare - everything would change. I don't know if we could handle it." But he continued to play for the fun of it, probably calculating that the chance of winning the jackpot was slim. In short, winning a lot of

money would result in an anomic situation, since the
financial challenge in his and his family's life was
built on the planning and saving up for future
projects instead of attaining them immediately.

Regularity and restrictions seem to imply
security. This is why Whyte sarcastically has
described budgetism as "the opium for the middle
classes":

The suburbanites have an almost obsessive desire
for regularity in money transactions ... Salary
checks, withholding deductions, mortgage payments -
the major items in middle-class finances - are
firmly geared to a thirty-day cycle, and so,
increasingly, are all the other items. It is,
suburbanites cheerfully explain, a matter of
psychology. They don't trust themselves ... In self-
entrapment is security. (1956:137)

Criminals, on the other hand, hold negative
opinions about regularities and restrictions of
money which for most of us seem to have a positive
value. Furthermore, criminals can afford these
values. They can live according to the principle of
adjusting income to expenses rather than the
reverse, since the cost of acquiring money for them
is quite low[1]:

You know, for you money is probably worth a lot,
but for me one thousand is like one hundred for
you ... I can always go out and buy me a Bacco
chisel and steal my money again...

Differences are also seen in what is meant by "large
sums", "moderate sums", "enough to get by on", etc.
A thief who has just told about a time where he had
spent what was then (in 1960) an ordinary one-year
salary in a couple of weeks is indignant about the
greediness of drug dealers.

"Drug dealers, they're only motivated by money,
they're just obsessed with money. They can earn a
million a year, which would be enough, but they
won't stop at that."

"You weren't crazy about money?"
"No, not as long as I had enough to get by."
"But 18,000?"
"Well, you can't help stumbling over it. After
that score I didn't do anything for two weeks.
Money goes quickly, you know. We bought some new
furniture and took a cab here, a cab there, and
party after party. You know, we drank five or six
bottles in a day, you were generous, and
cigarettes, soft drink and food ..."

Even though most of the inmates advocated the
"enough to get by on" philosophy, thieves did not
argue for equal incomes, nor did they react against
those with high incomes.

Table 34.   "It is quite all right that someone
earns a few hundred thousand crowns or
more a year."

%	Agree	Disagree	No opinion	Sum	N
Traditional thieves	47	44	9	100	(34)
Modern thieves	35	40	25	100	(40)
Mixed	26	47	26	100	(19)
Addicts	18	76	6	100	(17)
SIFO	34	51	16	100	(125)

"A few hundred thousand" is quite a high income in
Sweden, one which only a few earn. The answer
reflects the more entrepreneur-like attitude among
traditional thieves. Except for the addicts, the
other groups do not differ much from the SIFO
sample.

The scholars in the "new school of criminology"
believed that criminals oppose the unjust
capitalistic system.[2] According to the answers to
the question above, however, criminals as a group do
not form the avant-garde in a revolution for
equality. Some of the inmates stated in the informal

interviews that the reason for their being criminals was that they refused to accept a situation where they had to restrict themselves due to lack of funds. This is an answer that could be interpreted as "rebelling against the system", but in a very individualistic way.

Being a spendthrift

Criminals often describe themselves as being spendthrifts or not really caring about money. In a study from 1978, I got the following results:

Table 35.   "How would you describe your attitude towards money?"

%	Inmates
Thrifty, almost tight	2
Economical	13
Wasteful	51
Don't care about money, money doesn't mean that much	28
No answer	12
N	(101)

Note: More than one alternative was given by some of the respondents. Thus, the sum is greater than 100.

Compared to most ordinary people, inmates do have a more "easy come, easy go" attitude towards money.

Table 36.   "If you have some money left, you might as well spend it."

%	Agree	Disagree	No opinion	Sum	N
All inmates	40	43	17	100	(127)
SIFO	25	62	14	100	(125)

Actually, the differences are probably greater than the result shows. In the taped interviews, the

thieves told stories about spending-sprees and also
bragged a bit about these occasions. I have not
encountered the same attitude in similiar interviews
with non-criminals.

The following statement gave more disparity than
the question above:

Table 37.   "You might as well live on a day-to-day
             basis - that's how I reason when it
             comes to money."

%	Agree	Disagree	No opinion	Sum	N
Thieves	45	38	17	100	(76)
Addicts	11	56	33	100	(18)
All inmates	37	40	22	100	(114)
SIFO	11	77	11	100	(125)

This short-sighted economic planning among thieves
does not however mean that one is not interested in
money. As Simmel has pointed out in the article *The
Miser and the Spendthrift*, there is a similarity
between the two. The spendthrift is really as
interested in money as the miser, but the
spendthrift's interest is just hidden under a sort
of man-of-the-world attitude. His fascination with
money is expressed by the spending itself - this is
the important feature - not by an interest in the
objects which are bought. If one were indifferent
towards money, then throwing it away would be done
with indifference, not grandeur:

... the indifference about the value of money
which constitutes the essence and the carm of
prodigality is possible only because money is
actually treasured and assumed to be special.
(1971:183)

That money really does mean a lot despite the fact
that this is decisively denied is nicely illustrated
by a story in a biography about a thief. He recalls
a time when he and everybody else in a swank
roadhouse got their bills paid by a big spender. He
estimates the cost to about twenty thousand dollars,

and comments:

> That was a story in itself, that was an incident
> that I'll never forget. You know, after all, I was
> just a punk. I'd seen a great deal, I was older
> than my age, but I'll never forget that gesture of
> a bigshot. Not a petty bigshot, not anybody that
> wanted to just make an impression or anything, but
> a man that done things in a big way. (Martin,
> 1952:71)

Spending as a way of communicating success

According to Letkemann, criminals often display
successful scores by spending freely, offering
drinks, etc. to colleagues at bars known to be
criminal hang-outs. They do it in spite of the risk
that this might raise suspicion among the police or
informers, because: "Since by definition his work is
secret, it is he who must communicate his successes
and competence to others." (1973:45)

Adler and Adler notes in *The Irony of Secrecy in
the Drug World*, that although secrecy is of high
importance, drug dealers often neglect it, due to
some inherent qualities in their lifestyle. One of
these factors is that high prestige is given dealers
who handle large amounts of drugs. In order to
maintain their reputation, they reveal their
"secrets" by bragging or showing off in the fast
life of the dealing crowd. Similar to Letkemann, the
authors conclude about the dealer that:

Unless someone shares the knowledge of his
activities with others, there is no way he can get
the respect, fear, or admiration which he has earned
... (1980:259)

Money is furthermore one of the few measures of
status in the criminal's world. People in the
conventional world have more areas through which
they can attain respect or status: work, family, a
house, a new car, etc. The same argument can
probably explain the conspicuous consumption that
some criminals engage in. The way Suttles explains

why the blacks, in the slum that he studied, followed the ever-changing fashions is informative. He believes that they, in contrast to more established people, need this expressive style to get some kind of recognition and individualism:

Where persons are firmly entrenched in public statuses that are respected, trustworthy or powerful, they can afford the art of understatement, subtlety and modesty. With so many virtues it is easy to wait for someone else to point them out. Addams area Negroes are not so well placed. (1968:129)

Jackson points out still another aspect that makes thieves dependent on external means for status, namely the irregularity of their lifestyle. Contrary to prostitutes and addicts whose lifestyle implies more of long-term relationships with others such as customers, dope sellers, and the police, thieves are considered more isolated:

This relative isolation contributes to his dependence on externals for status, his tendency to spend money quickly and obviously, his attempt to make an expensive rather than "good" appearance. (1969:25)

Furthermore, the impossibility inherent in the criminal life to show off with, a luxurious car, a house , etc. (due to the inability to give a lawful account to questions from the police or taxation office) leads to squandering money in the present in order to achieve status and prestige.

Ideological reasons

This spending now, instead of saving for the future, seems to have an almost ideological meaning:

Whatever (money or drugs) become available are consumed in a conscious rejection of the normative middle-class value of saving. They live for the moment and let tomorrow worry about paying the tab. (Adler and Adler, 1980:461)

This ideological view towards consumption was expressed by the respondents in my study in statements such as "I want to be able to do what I want, when I want, and how I want." It is an attitude towards life that implies a denial of society's right to interfere with **my** wishes and an emphasis on the experiences here and how. Many said thing like "You only live once," meaning you have to make use of the opportunities you have when they arise.

> "You don't have any use for money that is bound up ... Money should be used, it's not to be kept somewhere ..."
> "Should it be used for living?"
> "Yeah, all the time. You don't know what day you're gonna die ... some people save and then they die, what's the use of that?"
> "What do you want to do with your money?"
> "Place it in the spenders' bank!! Parties and having a good time, go somewhere ..."

Another inmate talked about the squares' financial habits in the following derogatory way:

> "They'll go to Crete (a common destination for charter trips) and plan and ... changing cars, buying a Volvo and shit like that. They put an enormous amount of money into cars. You wouldn't think so, but they do. A lot of trash that they can't enjoy."
> "You think one should use money to have fun with or experience things with instead of just owning things?"
> "Yeah, right, but maybe they need another car, having a family and so on."
> "You don't?"
> "Well, not like that. I can have it for two months, then sell it and take a cab if I need to, instead. They can't. They are committed to keep on paying for it, monthly or whatever. I wonder how much fun it is, to me it sounds like too much routine ..."

Even if he recognizes the need for a car, he is

obviously sceptical about the gratification of a lifestyle that "forces" one to acquire a new Volvo.

Generosity

The interviewees often spoke about how they were able to give things away on the spur of the moment, be generous with friends, relatives, etc. This was said with a certain self-righteousness, distinguishing them from the squares, who had to save "every penny". It was a way of saying that money did not mean much, as well as expressing the ability to do things spontaneously. Analyzing this economically, one can see it as a result of the inability to save and invest inherent in their lifestyle: "You can't buy a house, unless you can explain where you got the money from." Analyzing generosity socially it can been seen as functional for the unity of the group. Goldberg, who has written about a drug community in Stockholm, describes the informal leader Richard as being very generous and comments:

He is not lending money, he is redistributing resources ... The giving and receiving of presents unifies the tribe under the leadership of the chief. (1973:84)

For the individual, being generous can also give a sense of having the upperhand and being in control. It is thus a sort of psychological-economical investment. In a study of hustlers, the author has bought one of the interviewees a drink at a bar. He is, however, not allowed to continue in the position of the one who is paying:

Immediately after I paid for the drink, he bought me another drink. I knew he wouldn't allow me to buy another drink, that he would never feel satisfied until he succeeded in getting me "charged". It was all a matter of status for Strode. It was his way of showing he had the money to back up his appearance. More generally his motto was: "Nobody should have anything over me." (Pryce,

1979:42)

Many of the inmates interviewed in my study had similar mottos. They said, for instance, "I don't allow anyone to control me," or summarizing their lives as "At least I don't owe anything to anyone." The last type of statement refers, of course, to being generally independent but this was often exemplified by not being in debt financially to any individual.

Being generous can also be seen as a sort of compensation - at least at some moments it is possible to be free with one's money, to get an upperhand in a situation. A man whom I would label as belonging to the "mixed" category, made this comment about living on social welfare:

> You feel bad living on welfare, that's not what you want to do. You don't want to take money and see it disappear in a few days. But it's impossible to make it last, budgeting for a long time, a week. So you waste it fast in a day or two and give away to those around you, undisciplined ...

Conspicuous consumption?

A few respondents described how they dressed conspicuously when they were out of prison, almost in the black pimp tradition, as this thief who described his attire:

> I used to dress in black and white and red ... I could wear white suits in the middle of the winter, a black shirt and a red scarf and a golden ring around the scarf. In any case, I would dress as expensively as possible.

This is very much in line with the decription of juvenile delinquents given by Matza and Sykes (1961). The authors compare these youngsters with Veblen's (1912) leisure elite and their taste for luxury and conspicuous consumption.

Most of the interviewees did not, however, belong to this group of consumers. In common with the non-addicted criminals was that they had a special style of consumption. Some said, for example, that they just wanted enough to get by. When asked about what "enough" was, they said things like "no luxuries". But when talking about consumption, they emphasized that they did not want to be restricted in things they wanted to buy or do. **This** seemed to be general but the things one wanted to do or buy shifted a lot. An example may illustrate what they meant:

"When do you hit life's jackpot? When are you happiest?"
"When you have enough to get by, when you enjoy yourself, and things work out ... as long as you can make ends meet. It's ridiculous to have high demands."

And he gives this as an example of what he wants to be able to do:

I was going home to my mother in Lund so I took a cab from Malmö. Well, she wasn't home so I invited the cab driver to a coffee shop for a cup of tea and suggested that we could wait there for a while till she came home. Sure, he said, and we went in and had something to eat and drink, had a beer and when we went back, she had returned. Things like that are nice to do ...

This is, of course, something that people on a regulated budget (cab fares are very expensive in Sweden) might see as highly irresponsible, economically. But for the respondent this was an example of the minor things in life that cheer you up. For him, conspicuous consumption was not as important as being able to do things when he decided he wanted to do them. He also emphasized the importance of being an individual. He exemplified this by saying that he could not understand why

people dressed just like everybody else. Since
others also talked about clothes as being so
important, I decided to test one of the statements
used in SIFO's lifestyle study on the inmates:

Table 38.   "I avoid dressing like everybody else."

%	Agree	Disagree	No opinion	Sum	N
Inmates	42	25	33	100	(127)
SIFO	24	42	34	100	(125)

The traditional thieves among the inmate sample
agreed most to this question - they were much less
concerned with conspicuous consumption than with
maintaining and cultivating their individualism.
Taylor (1982) even mentions an air of cultivated
"ordinariness" among professional criminals.
Individualism was important to my respondents
concerning their clothing but also in other areas.
Several of them had very definite opinions about
what kind of liquor they liked, favorite types of
food, ideas about interior decorating, special types
of furniture, etc.

Money as too important

That status is strongly connected to money might
also be experienced as troublesome. Many of my
respondents stated, for example, that "Money is the
only thing that counts here, you know." The qoute
below is from a thief who described himself as
having succeeded, earning respect by living on a
high standard. He was now, however, tired of the
all-importance of money in this world and saw this
as a reason for quitting crime. Anyhow, this is his
account of socializing in his former world:

... there were certain restaurants where you met
... it was not only the guests, but the staff and
the owner, and all, so everything was just "go
ahead" ... But then you're supposed to entertain

the people and show yourself in the right kind of clothes and have the right kind of chic, otherwise you weren't admitted anymore. So that's what counted ...

The third most frequent answer to a question about disadvantages in living as a criminal, given by 39% of the inmates, was that everything centered around getting money all the time. This is not - at least not entirely - a problem concerning the supply of money, since only 13% agreed to the alternative "bad finances". (See table 45.)

Finally, the quote below is very illustrative of money when experienced as too confining. A young hash dealer on his ambivalence both towards money and his criminal life:

It gets to the point where you spend money just to have a motivation to continue, because without that motivation you might as well quit.

9
LOOKING AT THE SQUARES

Comparisons with the square-johns

A way to get an identity is to compare oneself with others. Contrasts can help to provide a meaning in life and also to clarify alternatives.

"... each of us finds meaning in his life not only by identifying things for what they are, but also by noting what they are not. Moreover, in noting what they are not we clarify the alternatives that are open to us, thus establishing the psychological basis of what is most important of all - human freedom."[1]

In the interviews comparisons between the criminal life and that of the squares were a constantly reoccurring theme. Most of the time the criminal life won. This does not mean that the inmates saw the criminal life as the perfect life, but as Irwin (1980) has pointed out, a criminal life can be seen as more rewarding in the absence of other acceptable alternatives. The alternative as they see it is the negatively stereotyped lifestyle of the square-johns: their activities are dull, leisure means looking at TV, their outlook on life is narrow, they have experienced so little, etc. It is thought provoking that half of the inmates said "no" to the question "If you could choose now, would you prefer to live a square type of life?"

Shover points out that really committed and successful burglars even derive a psychological reward from the comparison with the squares:

Many **good burglars** derive feelings of satisfaction from a weighing of how their life compares with the lives they believe are experienced by many **square johns.** When they take into account their incomplete education and lack of job skills, the only alternative legitimate role which they can imagine as being open to them is one which they evaluate with extreme negativism. They know it as the **working stiff,** a name which, by itself, tells worlds. (1971:122)

This negative outlook is well known in the criminological literature. Here, however, I wish to examine this attitude a bit more extensively than is usually done.

In a question from a study of mine in 1978, the inmates were asked if they thought that the life of the squares contained anything positive. Of the 88 respondents, more than a third categorically stated "no", while the rest mentioned some aspects as being attractive, such as having a family, a job, or a more secure life. There is thus not a total negativism against the lifestyle of the squares. The result of another question in a later study about who gets the most appreciation and most respect in the criminal world agrees with this. A fourth of those interviewed felt that the one who could earn his money illegally but at the same time live like the average man had the most respect. That is, he had really been able to beat the system, arrange a front and avoid having too many of the insecurities of the criminal life. For example, a young addict and thief wanted to straighten up in the following, unexpected way:

"I used to say this life is worth it even if I'm only out three months a year. I live those months much more than the working stiffs. But I've changed and now I don't think it's true."

"Are you going to live like the working stiffs
now?"
"No, I don't think I can take a nine-to-five job.
My body hasn't got that in its computer ... No, I
have to straighten out and put things into some
kind of order. I've been inside here too long. I
can start dealing drugs but you can't organize
that if you're an addict yourself, it's just not
possible ... And if that doesn't work out, I can
start studying and get a job."

Why the squares are looked down on

Boring life

Table 39.   "What would be the disadvantages if you
were to live a square lifestyle?"

%	Inmates
Difficulties in establishing contact with the squares	20
Problems with finances	35
Miss my friends	14
Miss drugs	5
Miss partying	10
Boring life, no excitement	72
N	(117)

What do the inmates feel is negative about living
like the squares? First of all, as seen above, the
main criticism is that they find the squares' life
boring: no thrills or adventures. The spectre of the
regularity of this type of life is more terrifying
than the thought of doing time, as is seen in the
biography of a thief:

The alternative - the prospect of vegetating the
rest of my life in a steady job, catching the 8.13
to work in the morning, and the 5.50 back again at
night, all for ten or fifteen quid a week - now
that really terrify (sic.) me, far more than the

thought of a few years in the nick. (Parker and Allerton, 1962:88)

Part of the negative attitude towards the Joneses comes from their being seen as prisoners in their way of life - that they cannot imagine anything outside their own lifestyle. Criminals want more in terms of experiences than what an ordinary life seems to offer:

"Do you enjoy having done things like that, that are a bit odd, unusual, compared to most people' experiences?"
"Yeah, they have fun in their way, I guess. Maybe they think back on old family stories, I don't know, but ... Maybe I want a bit more, and I do get more, living as I do."

Due to the Joneses' taken-for-granted, routine-like lives, they lack "hope" for finding anything better:

I've got something that most guys, especially the Joe Squares, don't have. I've got hope! I've got the streets, and I'm going out there again. I've got something to look forward to. Joe Square has the rut, the routine, and there's no hope for him. When I get out there again I can make up for everything that is happening to me now. I'll be free, free to live the way I want and to do what I want. I can shoot dope, steal, rob, pimp whores. I can live as fast and as good as I want. (Manocchio and Dunn, 1970:33)

Naive and "imprisoned"

Another criticism is that the ordinary man is sometimes "naive". This, however, can also be advantageous when doing business: they will not cheat you. Some of the respondents said in a slightly condescending tone that they are nice, but not smart, and they are grateful:

They're good, the workers, good to do business with, never any problems. They'll pay and that's it ... they're grateful, you know, and it's nice somehow when people are grateful.

Coupled with this is the theme that the squares are also a type of prisoner, of conventional and formal rules. Being a prisoner of conventionalism is expressed in statements such as "They care so much about what others think of them." The other major theme is that they are trapped in "the system".

"I just can't see why ordinary people don't see through the system. They'll work their ass off and they'll die before retiring ..."
"You think that they adjust ...?"
"They are driven into a trap and then they can't get away from it. They get stuck with a family, having kids and a job, and after that, you know ..."

They are also seen as conforming, without resistance, even to clearly unfair treatment:

Of course we need laws and I'm prepared to follow them, but in that case I want something in exchange. Because I don't think the laws are proportioned to the individual's right to live. Look at the squares, like if he wants to get drunk on Saturday night, he can get thrown in a cell, beaten by the police, and he takes it! What kind of life is that? Then you might as well be in prison. At least there are clear boundaries here, because they'll lock you up. And then you can have your Christmas when you get out ...

Bad finances

Thirty-five percent of the inmates' answers about negative features in the squares' lifestyle concerned bad finances. (See table 45) Through low pay, bad living arrangements, mortgages, etc. they

are considered to be financially harassed. This view
often derives from the interviewees' own experiences
of problems at times when they tried to go straight.
Just the thought of being forced to plan a household
budget is repellant:

> "Of course you can get yourself a woman and kids
> and move out to Rosengård (a suburban housing
> area) and get yourself a job and get stuck in one
> of those cells. It's a cell-system just like the
> prison, but you see, I'm not interested in that
> kind of thing. That's not happiness to me. I tried
> it for a while but it was only worries and bills
> and problems. And to have to plan your ... what in
> hell are you planning for? Well, it ended up
> planning to make ends meet."
> "You planned your household finances?"
> "Yeah, and that's nothing I want to keep doing,
> it's crazy ... I don't think that anyone should
> have more time left over if you're going to work
> and have a family. You should be better off ... If
> that's the way it's going to be, I think it's
> better just drifting around ..."

Envy

Due to their restricted economy, the squares are
said to be envious of each other. The criminals'
picture of the ordinary man is thus in line with the
general view of him as being much concerned with
"keeping up with the Joneses"[2]:

> "Most workers are envious of each other. If one of
> them has something, the other one wants the same."
> "Aren't you?"
> "No, you know we have the same opportunities."

Envy is even said to be the "real" reason for why
the police "won't leave you alone":

> I was really determined to quit, on a larger scale
> anyway, just having small "jobs" earning some

money. But the police won't leave you alone -
there's such envy: "How can you afford to go out
to restaurants?", etc. ...

Lack of nerve

Quite a few of the inmates believed that many
squares really wished to do what they, the
criminals, had done, if only they dared. Thus,
Polsky (1969) warns students dealing with deviants
to be aware of their assumption that the students
want to be like them, and the only thing holding
them back is their lack of nerve. A young thief even
generously offered to exchange jobs with an ordinary
man one week at a time. The respondents decided,
however, that the project would flop due to the
latter's being too scared:

> I don't dislike them, but I feel sorry for them.
> They live all their lives toiling and wearing
> themselves out, complaining about their jobs and
> their bosses and they never get any money, can
> only take a month of vacation a year ... Of course
> someone has to do that. Maybe one could take
> turns, you know, he'd be at the factory a week,
> and I, one week. Nice thought but unfortunately
> unrealistic, maybe ... But they might not have the
> nerve anyway, they get nervous just getting twelve
> scores (out of thirteen) in the soccer betting -
> it could have been thirteen (laughter).

Just dreaming about the things one wants to do is
looked down upon in general:

> And their talk ... the man, if you can get down to
> it, he always "fancies" the woman next door, but
> of course he never gets around to actually doing
> her. It's frightening, it's chronic. At least
> criminals have something interesting to talk
> about, their talk is deeper and more real, the
> life they lead goes at a much faster tempo and has
> got more excitement in it. (Parker and Allerton,

1962:109)

A condescending view

Criminals are often portrayed as either wanting deep down to be like ordinary people, or regarding them with hostility and bitterness.

McKorkle and Korn (1954) write about "a rejection of the rejectors", and Sykes and Matza (1957) have described one of the neutralizing techniques used by juvenile delinquents as "condemnation of the condemners". The authors use words like bitterness, and describe the psychological function of reversing a negative attitude: "... by attacking others, the wrongfulness of his own behavior is more easily repressed or lost to view." Cohen (1955) makes a similar conclusion in his work about the subculture of juvenile delinquents. Since they "really" want a middle class type of life, due to influences from school and the rest of society, they react with frustration and hostility to their own lower class living conditions.

I have however not found that such attitudes of bitterness and hostility are common. An attitude of superiority or condescention seems to be more accurate. Gibbons description of thieves' attitudes towards straight people is illustrative:

Thieves tend not to demonstrate hostility toward any of these individuals; instead they simply regard themselves as different from, and superior to, these others. (1968:247)

The quotes given earlier in this chapter confirm this attitude; the relative frequency of the answers to the question in table 40 illustrates it further.

The most common answer is "I like him, he is okay, I guess". Many, however, after answering this added things like "It's admirable that they don't give up", "Society can't exist without them", "They've got a nice attitude - go to work and be pleased with what they've got". These statements demonstrate a condescending attitude rather than bitterness or expressions of frustration, as some criminologist have claimed as typical.

Table 40. "What is your opinion about the
          ordinary working guy?"

%	Inmates
He does not dare to live, he is boring	27
He is so suspicious about everything	16
He knows so little about our life	41
He does not like people like us	25
I like him, he is okay, I guess	44
N	(122)

In further support of my view, as seen in table 41a,
of the inmates who found it difficult to talk to
ordinary people, only 6% attributed this to not
liking them.

The stereotype derived from society

A negative view from society

The negative view of squares' lifestyle is in some
ways taken from other parts of society. Firstly, I
think it is equalled in much of what is published in
newspapers, books, etc., by "professional debaters"
and authors, discussion shows on television, and so
on. Also, as the criminologist Laurie Taylor (1971)
has pointed out, some sociologists like Durkheim,
Sorokin and Zimmerman have described "the lower
class" existence in the industrial world as
monotonous, and claimed that these people are
reduced to mere objects.
    The second source of experiencing their lives as
exciting and special lies in the attention that
criminals get. The thieves talked, for example,

about "reading the reviews" after committing a crime. Addicts today might get even more publicity and are seen as an even more deviant and special group than the thieves. Waldorf gives this attention from society as one reason why addicts feel they belong to such an interesting group:

Society's heavy and abiding concern and the flurry of police activity are often interpreted by the addict as evidence of heroin's importance and power. The reasoning is often thus: "If heroin is **not** such an important and powerful drug, why is society so concerned about it? They enact all these laws and put us in jail because they themselves are afraid of it." Being illegal, makes the drug attractive in the eyes of many, and the cat-and- mouse-game with the police, makes drug-seeking by the addict an exciting and dramatic activity ... This is, I am sure, the basis for the addict's belief that he is leading a far more different and exciting life than the square. (1973:16)

Criminals also sense that people have a somewhat romantic attitude towards those who lead such an unusual life; this enhances their way of seeing themselves as leading a less boring life than the rest of us. The practice of selling things by telling people that goods are stolen, i.e. pretending a false gold chain is real, stolen gold, can be viewed in this light. That this method is successful is probably not only due to people believing they are making a smart deal. By buying something illegal, people can get a feeling of being part of something that is a bit fascinating due to its secretness.

Experiencing "more" as a criminal

In everyday life the concept of 'experience' often has the connotation of something odd or new. A man or a woman is said to be experienced in the field of love if he or she has had many relationships, as opposed to one long one, learning, maybe, different and more subtle things.

Criminals often picture themselves as adventurers, as is shown later on in this work, and as such they derive a feeling of being closer to real life and experiencing "more". Simmel has pointed out that the adventurer:

... makes a system of life out of his life's lack of system, when out of his inner necessity he seeks the naked, external accidents and builds them into that necessity. (1971:191)

The interviewed criminals often talked about themselves as "really having lived", and having experiences, as opposed to ordinary people. I guess that the basis for this is what was said above, experiences that are a bit odd or unusual compared to those that most of us acquire.

If I'd been a working stiff, I don't think I would have **lived**, not like I have. And had the chance to take drugs and drink and have lots of buddies. Got to know lots of unusual, interesting guys, ya know. I've seen a lot, done a lot ...

The way criminals regard "real life" as opposed to most people's everyday life with all its conventions has a societal background and is shared with other groups. Shils, in his book *Tradition*, makes the following comment:

Traditions of respectability and hypocrisy repressed "true individuality" and stood in way for life ... The "cry for life" was just not a slogan of a socialistic propagandist; it was deeper. It was a cry for an unknown object called "life" because life was held to be antithetical to custom and convention. Many less intellectuals and many less cultivated persons, too, were bored by what they received. Society seemed too cut and dried, too much the same thing ... (1981:235)

Unusual, often "heavy" experiences are also seen as giving a specially valid knowledge of life, not the ordinary practical everyday type but one that transcends the commonplace.

I once met a manager of a very sleazy hotel

occupied by addicts and prostitutes. Earlier, he had
had a middle-class job, but quit this after a
divorce. The way he looked at his present situation
was in terms of wanting to get out of it, but at the
same time appreciating the experiences it had given
him. "I haven't learned as much during my whole life
as during these two years when I've been down here
in this skid-row." It is an interesting attitude,
since the knowledge he gets under his present
circumstances is something that may be difficult to
translate if he returns to middle-class life.

An ex-criminal views his former life in a similar
light:

> One thing that's good with such a life, if it
> doesn't break you, is that you learn how to take
> care of yourself. Nobody picks you up if you fall
> ... If you fall you'll hurt yourself real bad. The
> experience that I now have of life and of people,
> that's the most precious thing I own. 'Cause it
> hasn't all been bad, I've learnt a lot about how
> it **really** is.

This is of course knowledge that they feel the
squares lack. A young man's description of his view
of the squares as being untroubled and seeking
perfection:

> "First of all, he doesn't know anything."
> "About what?"
> "About the world. He kind of lives inside a shell
> with white inner-walls, and he scrubs and polishes
> them to make 'em even whiter, even more bright and
> shining."

Different experiences

Experiencing different things does not only imply a
sort of superior attitude from the inmates in that
they felt that they experienced "more" but also led
to difficulties in communication with the average
guy. As can be seen in the table below, they

emphasize that the difficulties in talking with squares lie in not sharing the same experiences.

Table 41. "Do you find it difficult at times to talk to ordinary people?"

%	Inmates
Yes, sometimes	60
No, seldom	40
Total	100
N	(138)

Table 41a. "If yes, why?"

%	Inmates
Difficult to find things to talk about	46
We do not share the same experiences	46
I cannot tell them about my life	31
Ordinary people do not like people like me	38
I do not like them	6
N	(72)

The quote below is illustrative of the subtleties in everyday life that can be difficult if one has different outlooks on the world:

> I've worked as a cab-driver, but I don't like it. They're a pain in the ass. A lot of drunks. Drunks talk, I can't take it ... the boss at the job, and the old lady at home, I don't see that as particularly interesting. It's none of my business. I'm not interested in 'em, and why should I be?

This man saw himself as having been through a lot

and the events of his customers, quarrelling with
the boss and the wife, being drunk, etc., somehow
seemed petty and definitely alien to his own
concerns. Not only the problems of the squares but
also their definition of risk seems petty for
criminals. The cab-driver above also told about
events that his customers thought were daring and
exciting, such as being drunk on ordinary working
days or flirting with unknown women, things which he
would not deign to call "risks". Since criminals are
accustomed to taking risks this often lead to a lack
of understanding towards the concerns of ordinary
people.

As Goffman has noted, "different individuals and
groups have somewhat different personal base-lines
from which to measure risk and opportunity; a way of
life involving much risk may cause the individual to
give little weight to a risk that someone else might
find forbidding." (1967:157-158)

Not sharing the same experiences and problems also
gives rise to practical considerations in making
conversation with the squares since the groups do
not speak "the same language":

"I find it hard to communicate with the square-
johns, it's like we don't have the same interests
... we haven't experienced the same things ... If
I start at a new job, I can't tell 'em 'bout my
break-ins, about who I've been seeing and ..."
"So what do they speak about?"
"... Their work and their family ... my kid's got
two teeth now, and stuff like that ... And the
vacation last year, you know. What damn vacation?"
(laugh)

The difficulties are, of course, not only practical,
these different experiences and interests also cause
lacks of intimacy, relaxation and spontaneity,[3]
since small talk becomes problematic:

Just take you and I together here, for instance,
you get acquainted with me someplace and like me,

so we go out to dinner or something together and I
have to keep avoiding you. See, just little tiny
normal questions that you would ask another guy
wihtout any thought and he would answer without
any thought. But I have to cover up so I have to
continuously stay on my toes and I can't enjoy a
square-john's company. (Chambliss and King,
1972:76)

A similar example is given by Martin, who has
written about the thief Gene. The author recalls how
he invited Gene to his suburban home during
weekends, and how he reacted with unease when the
author's friends dropped in:

I noticed that he was not entirely at ease around
them. He had been so long away from the company of
non-criminal people ... You would think him rather
dull because he wouldn't be very talkative. Most
of his interests involve crime and he cannot talk
crime to laymen; and as for small talk ,it is a
little hard to make small talk if everything
reminds one of crime, as it does to him. The other
day during a lull in conversation he pointed to my
type-writer and said 'I know a fellow makes a
living stealing them ...' (1952:5)

On the other hand, differing experiences can of
course be rewarding. Some of the interviewees
expressed a wish to see people in their free time
who were not criminals, since they had enough shop
talk in prison. Others stated that they wanted to
talk about more general things such as politics,
society-related questions, etc., that their criminal
friends did not know too much about.

Going straight and yet not straight
– the third alternative

So far we have mainly examined the negative features
of the squares' lifestyle as seen by the
interviewees. In order to see whether this

alternative held any attraction, I posed the following question:

Table 42.   "What are the advantages in the lifestyle of the ordinary man?" (%)

%	Inmates
You meet other kinds of people	24
Better finances	18
The family appreciates it	24
Get away from drugs	13
Get away from liquor	15
More interesting life	18
Don't have to spend time in prison	72
N	(118)

It is interesting that the only statement about the
squares' lives that really got any response was
"Don't have to spend time in prison". If one
considers this rather negative view, it is natural
that those who want to quit look for a third
alternative - something inbetween the criminal world
and the squares' world.[4] The results of the question
below show the wish for the third alternative.

Table 43.   "If you are not planning to live as a
criminal in the future, what type of
life can you consider living?"

%	Inmates
That of an ordinary square-john	21
Support myself legally, but not live like the square-john	72
There is no style of life outside the criminal world that would suit me	7
Sum	100
N	(138)

What this third alternative meant, however, seemed

hard to define. There was space left in the questionnaire, where they could add what they meant by "Support myself legally, but not live like the square-johns". Very few did, however, which I think mirrors the difficulty many have in envisioning something apart from the two worlds which they knew about - the criminal and the square. This is especially interesting, I think, since we are living in a time where many alternative ways of living are made possible.

Some, however, described alternatives in the taped interviews. A young inmate spoke, for example, about a friend who worked as a delivery man whose hours were fairly free: he could take time off, smoke some pot in a park before continuing, and have free afternoons - not working nine-to-five. This was something the interviewee saw as a possible alternative.

The main reason for quitting crime seems to be due to a 'burning-out' effect, or that criminal life in itself can become boring. Shover (1971) noted that precisely that which was considered an advantage in the criminal world can become boring: too much leisure , too many late nights, too much gambling and entertainment, and for some, too much drugs. This, as I see it, can become just as much routine as any other experience in any other type of life and can thus create a wish for new life alternatives. A few quotes to illustrate:

"You said you wanted to quit because this life has become boring?"
"Yeah, I've been doing this for ten or twelve years now and then you wanna try something new. Because I've done this thing and it gets to be the same experience time after time. The same things happen, so it starts to get boring."

Another:

"Is this life exciting?"
"Yeah, it has been fun a lot of times, trying, but

> fun at many times. Fun episodes."
> "Is that a factor that makes you keep on?"
> "No, no, I don't know why. It gets to be a sort of
> routine ..."

It is thus important to note that it is often not
because of moral reasons that one wants to quit:

> "You said you want to change your lifestyle?"
> "Crime doesn't turn me off, it's far from that.
> But then you have to weigh pros and cons, what's
> most important. I'm just as criminal as I've
> always been, it's just that I've found more
> important things in life."
> "What?"
> "Well, you mature. You get to be interested in new
> things. This is really a narrow world. It's as
> petty as the squares'. It's the same damned talk,
> and the same way of being all the time. In ninety-
> nine cases out of a hundred, it's the same type of
> people. There ain't no **personal** exhange."

A new life then, requires other and different
activities than the ones they have experienced but
at the same time not be defined as "square" and
boring. Finally, a quote that illustrates both the
importance of a third alternative and the
difficulties in quitting if one does not know what
to do outside criminal life:

> What's the damn meaning in sitting in a place and
> tilting a chair? Going to the employment office,
> looking for jobs you hardly ever get? At best you
> get hold of a TV, and sit there and brood in front
> of it with a beer ... You need some kind of
> stimulation.

This guy had tried at times to get some friends
(criminals) to go with him to sport events, but they
just laughed at him, because this was 'square'
stuff. Since he did not have any other friends, this
effort of doing "something else" had thus not

succeeded – an illustration of tiny things having a symbolic value and importance but which are still obviously so difficult.

10
REWARDS

Descriptions and analyses of criminals have often emphasized the negative features of their lives. However, in order to increase the understanding of why some people get involved with criminality and perhaps even more why they stay involved, it is important to also recognize the attractions of crime.

It has been argued that we have neglected to study the rewards of crime and that this might be due to a view of the deviant as being forced into crime because of intense situational or structural pressure.[1] The latter perspective appertains especially to scholars in the theoretical school of subcultures.[2] In contrast those who made empirical studies of delinquent gangs, Thrasher (1927) in particular, described a reality of excitement, adventure and the role of romanticism for gang boys. Bordua made this comment concerning the different types of analyses:

Thrasher's boys enjoyed themselves being chased by the police, shooting dice, skipping school, rolling drunks. - Cohen's boys and Cloward and Ohlin's boys are driven by grim economic and psychic necessity into rebellion. It seems peculiar that modern analysts have stopped assuming that 'evil' can be fun and see gang delinquency as arising only when boys are driven away from 'good'. (1961:136)

Some modern criminologists have, however, pointed to different positive aspects of a criminal lifestyle. Polsky has, for example, made the following comment on the attractiveness of crime:

Indeed, one of the most genuinely appealing things about crime to career criminals and part-timers alike - though one would hardly gather this from criminology texts - is that for most crimes the working hours are both short and flexible. (1969:103)

Nettler (1972), among others, has written about the economic rewards, which will be discussed further below. Shover points out the psychological rewards that "the good burglar" gets when he compares himself with square johns, whom he views as the personification of the exploited and alienated industrial man. Burglars tend to view their own lives as better and even see them in a bit of a romantic light, especially when they compare them with legal working experiences often in dull, low-paid jobs. They point out that they have free working hours, freedom from supervision and a challenging life:

Unlike the **working stiff** he can realize himself in his work; there is unparallelled opportunity for inventiveness and creativity; the work **is** challenging. (1971:124)

In my study, I tried to determine how the respondents viewed the advantages and disadvantages of crime by posing the questions cited in table 44 and 45.

The money factor

Money was stated as the main advantage of a criminal life by the interviewees: 51% mentioned this. Only 13% saw "bad finances" as a drawback in their criminal lifestyle.

Table 44.   "What types of advantages are there in
             living as a criminal?"

%	Inmates
You have more money (at least at times)	51
You are more independent	48
You have more freedom (outside the pen)	36
Avoid working exact hours	35
There is more excitement	33
You meet more interesting people	28
N	(92)

Note: The only difference among the groups is the
         money item, which 67 % of traditional thieves
         mention which is more than the other groups.

Table 45.   "What types of disadvantages are there
             in living as a criminal?"

%	Inmates
Too much time in jail	50
This life is too hard	44
Your whole life revolves around just getting money all the time	39
You're not accepted by society	36
It's hard to build a family	29
Monotonous in the long run	28
Too much drugs	28
Too much alcohol	22
Too much violence	15
Bad finances	13
N	(116)

Lately, crime has been discussed in terms of
economical rationality.[3] Nettler notes, discussing
the rationality of crime as a preferred career, that
many crimes against property "represent a consciously adopted way of making a living" (1978:185). The

author notes further about successful thieves:

Given the low risk of penalty and the high probability of reward, given the absence of pangs of guilt and the presence of hedonistic preferences, crime is a rational occupation. (1978:186)

Crime as a means of supporting oneself is especially valid for the "able criminal" who actually makes more money than he would in the law-abiding occupations that would be open to him, and his expenditures and style of life are high even by ordinary standards.[4]

Economic rationality as discussed here was expressed in my interviews by those who argued against thieves being proud of their work skills. For the professional, who lives on crime, money is the goal:

> It's not the satisfaction of being able to open a safe nicely, but it's what might be in it that's important.

However, as Nettler points out, crime does not need to be successfully carried out in order to be rational. For those with small opportunities in other spheres of life, crime might be a more rewarding alternative than, say, a low-paid job or unemployment due to lack of contacts or education. Thus, even if you are a loser, or if you are not in the higher echelon, criminality might provide you with a better financial situation. One respondent, even though he had been rather a failure as a thief, still said, "I've never been so broke in my life as when I was working." (Shover, 1971:123)

Similarly, a young addict and petty thief in my study claimed that he always had money until he quit drugs. A few of those I interviewed who had gone straight a long time before felt that the biggest problem in the beginning was that of their finances. For example, they could no longer buy a pair of stolen jeans for a quarter of the regular price.

Economic rationality can also be seen in the norm of those criminals who state that if you cannot earn

good money in crime, you should not be in this kind
of business. Otherwise, you might as well earn your
money legally.

> I don't feel that it's worth stealing just to
> live. I can **earn** enough money to live. (Martin,
> 1952:272)

One of my respondents stated the same: one should
really earn more than in other types of work, given
the risks of criminality. At the same time, however,
he reflected on the long-term rationality and said
that in the long run, crime costs too much if
"wasted time" is considered:

> I don't like any type of work ... You can't work
> daytime if you're living like this ... no chance.
> You'll have to decide one or the other. But if you
> can't support yourself on the night shifts you
> might as well quit. So you should earn more
> really, some don't. But in a way it's always a
> loss, it's a lot of years down the drain, that you
> won't get back. But you never think about that
> when you're outside.

It is thus important to note that rationality as
seen by the actor differs in different situations.
When the criminal is out of prison, surrounded by
illegal opportunities which at that time look
promising, crime looks rational. In prison, however,
things might look different.

Glaser (1964) has shown that prisoner's careers
often follow a zigzag pattern. When they get out,
they often try a legitimate job and if this after
some time fails or is not seen as satisfying, they
return to crime. Success, however, seemed to evoke
repetition, whether in legitimate or illegitimate
pursuits. Success might be especially important in
the beginning of a criminal career. It might even
determine whether one will continue or not:

> When we started with our first robbery, if it

hadn't been successful we would probably have quit. A lot of times people will hit a place and just get $40 or $50. We got $200 on the first time. (Jackson, 1972:40)

Monetary success at a "job" might confirm one's commitment to crime if one has previously been "drifting".[5] The story told by an older thief about how he began with crime is illustrative. He told me how he used to hang around guys who stole, when he was young, but only worked as a look-out for them. Then, after a few years, he did his first job because he was short of money at the time:

"I told my girl I'd go out for a while. And I only brought my screwdriver and bicycled to a car firm, smashed the window and I was so damn lucky ... I'd never been to the firm and go right up to the safe. I looked at it and thought 'It's nothing to bother with, with a small screwdriver.' I began to look in the desk and found the key to the safe in the upper drawer! There was 18,000 crowns (at the time a normal one-year salary) in the box!"
"Really?"
"Yeah" (laughter) "more than 18,000 crowns. Like that, it's not difficult to become a thief."

Furthermore, the successful completion of a deviant act might of course also reduce a person's doubt or fears and thus increase the possibility of repetition.

Challenges and thrills

The big disadvantage of the square-john lifestyle was that it was considered boring. Living as a criminal, on the other hand, often meant the reverse - fun, excitement, etc., not only concerning criminal acts but also in one's leisure time.[6] Kicks and thrills are however not necessarily seen as attractions by all groups:
    ... there are many good reasons to take comfort in

... uneventfulness and seek it out, voluntarily foregoing practical gambles along with risk and opportunity ... The question is one of security. (Goffman 1967:174)

Criminals, however, to a higher extent than most ordinary people can be described as action-seekers. An illustration of this is the difference with which criminals and conventional people look upon chance-taking:

Table 46.   "I enjoy taking chances."

%	Agree	Disagree	No opinion	Sum	N
Inmates	46	32	22	100	(115)
SIFO	26	52	22	100	(125)

Taking chances is, of course, a way for the criminals to achieve challenges and thrills. Even fear can be thrilling. Lofland (1969) has, for example, discussed what he calls "pleasant fearfulness" in crime. An illustration from my interviews:

"Can't it be boring to steal?"
"Well, figure for yourself, when you're doing something exciting, something you think is exciting, you wanna do that again, right?"
"Doesn't it get too exciting and make you nervous?"
"When you hear tut tut (police car sirens), and they come after you, oh, it's fun as hell, you drive all around town having those blue lights after you, around the streets. Oh, I'm criminal, you can hear that" (laughter). "Don't let any social worker listen to this..."

Pleasant fearfulness must however be seen as manageable in order to be experienced as pleasant. This sense of something being manageable is connected to the experience of mastering something, a job or a situation. The quote below from a young thief illustrates some factors that "lure" one into a criminal life and perhaps keep one there, such as knowing that one masters something.

"How about excitement?"
"There's a lot to that, that's right. For me, anyway. You get an outlet for many things in that way."
"Through stealing, or the whole life?"
"The stealing in itself, the act. I really liked it...you know that you can do something really good... it's my thing."
"To succeed or not?"
"Yeah, succeeding... you feel successful somehow if you make it. I guess everybody wants to experience that, one way or another... So it wasn't only the money."

It should be added that experiencing crime as fun evidently derives from the fact that crime is crime, i.e., the act of disregarding prohibitions can in itself be a thrill. As Lofland points out, this has probably little to do with attitudes of right or wrong in the actor; it is, rather, knowing that others see these acts as wrong:

The sense of adventure probably derives, in part, from the knowledge that **others** define the act as wrong, not from unequivocally believing so oneself. (1969:107)

Stealing and planning of crime

Young inmates regarded stealing itself as a thrill. Table 47 shows the answers to a question from my study in 1978.

Even though the numbers are small, I think the tendency of the younger thieves to see stealing as exciting is quite general. The older inmates' appreciation of risk-taking was a bit different from that of the younger ones. The older respondents seemed to view crime more in the light of business or work.

Table 47.   "Stealing creates a kind of excitement
             in life"

| % | Age | | |
	-24	25-34	35-
Agree	70	36	25
Disagree	11	38	67
No opinion	19	27	8
	---	---	---
	100	100	100
N	(27)	(45)	(12)

The following is a quote from a biography
illustrating how crime tends to become interpreted
as business as one gets older. To a question about
why he became a criminal:

> ... I could say it was because I'd always had a
> desire for adventure, for living dangerously. That
> was true when I was young, but it isn't true now,
> and I still go on. Now crime's just business,
> that's all. (Parker and Allerton 1962:106)

This change in the reason for staying in crime might
be due to the fact that the experiences gained from
committing criminal acts are no longer new for the
older respondents and thus no longer adventures.
Crime can however still be a challenge. While the
younger thieves think the act of stealing is
exciting, the older ones see planning and out-
mastering the police as the challenge:

> "Can't stealing be exciting or fun?".
> "Yeah, sure. Some see it as a sport, to measure
> one's strength against the police's. Not the
> individual policeman, but the whole organization
> which you shouldn't underrate, their
> possibilities... Jesus!"
> "Can it be fun even for those of you who have been
> at it for a long time?"

"Yeah, sure." (laughter) "Sure, it can be fun..."

Furthermore, the calculation of risks rather than the execution of a project can be interpreted as a challenge. An older thief, more thoughtful than the former:

"The excitement can be due to all that goes with it, how to weigh a situation."
"Strategy?"
"Yeah, you have to have a whole system for making it... so you can be very quick in situations where it's important to act."

After the challenge is met, one has an immediate sense of accomplishment, which is perhaps more than what many other occupations offer. The well-known jazz musician Art Pepper describes his elation after his first successful attempt in crime:

I felt so happy. I had never felt any elation like that before. It was a feeling of power, a feeling of accomplishment. I really felt like a man. I looked at the other people on the streets and I thought, "They ain't nothing compared to me! I'm a giant! King Pepper! King Arthur! Mr. Jazz! Mr. Everything!" (Pepper, 1979:232)

The sense of accomplishment that Pepper wrote about is of course related to the importance of the rewards of knowing a job, a reward that after a while becomes a sense of "being in control."[7]

Other thrills

Action-seeking seems to affect the way criminals tend to spend their leisure:
Many criminals gamble constantly and heavily at horse races or in games among themselves. Con men, who might be expected to avoid dishonest gambling games often lose their money on the "other man's game"... There is some reason to believe that a

fairly close connection exists between the
recreational interests of criminals and their
deviant behavior ... It is possible that public and
supervised recreation comes to symbolize values in
direct opposition to those of the habitual or
professional criminal. (Lemert, 1951:329)

As Lemert points out, the choice of leisure
activities such as gambling or hanging out at bars
or pool halls, etc. that have somewhat of a "bad"
atmosphere might have a symbolic value. In Sweden
gambling clubs are illegal; this is probably why, in
my opinion, many of the interviewees especially
wanted to emphasize that they often went to these
places - telling me they knew their whereabouts.
Gambling with big amounts of money adds of course to
the excitement and creates action:

> We're drawn to gambling, ya' know, it's like ya'
> stand in front of slot machines and such... it
> could happen that six hundred, a thousand crowns
> (around $100) could vanish every night... Once I
> had ten thousand going in a gambling club that the
> cops busted later on... I was playing on five
> machines at once, running from the one to the
> other all the time...

In a comparison of different gambling activities,
more of the inmates played roulette, bingo, pool and
horses than the control group. In reply to a
question about whether they played cards for money,
30 % of the inmates agreed that they often did this,
as compared to 9 % of the control group.
Furthermore, a fourth of the inmates had won, lost
or been in games where the stakes had been $100-200,
compared to 2 % of the control group.[8]

It can be added that the respondents described
themselves as "gamblers" not only in the literal
sense as described above but also in a more general
way. This is of course connected with the love of
chance-taking discussed previously.

However, it is not only specific leisure
activities such as gambling that criminals prefer to

be exciting but also the people with whom they associate.

Table 48.   "I prefer friends who are exciting and
              do things one doesn't expect."

%	Agree	Disagree	No opinion	Sum	N
Inmates	52	19	29	100	(127)
SIFO	32	40	27	100	(125)

There also seems to be a general wish for **new** experiences, which for example can be seen in the following result:

Table 49. "I enjoy eatingat new, exotic
          restaurants."

%	Agree	Disagree	No opinion	Sum	N
Inmates	59	24	17	100	(127)
SIFO	39	46	16	100	(125)

Adventure

Associated with gambling is the lust for adventure. The meaning of adventure implies experiencing new and perhaps unusual activities or situations. The thief can be described as a kind of "adventurer". Many of the thieves talked with a certain pride about how they had done almost "everything". It seems to be the general consensus in the group that one should gain "experiences", especially as a youngster:

When I was young I used to go bumming around during the summers. I was a sailor for a while and worked at an amusement park for some time. Most of the time I used to hitchhike or walked the roads, even if I had money for the train fare: I preferred it, you have to try some different things... 'Cause then you won't have to sit around

when you're old telling yourself I should have
done this or that. And now I enjoy taking it easy.

As has already been pointed out, crime might acquire
more of a business atmosphere than one of excitement
when one gets older. However, as Thrasher suggested,
one can become accustomed to adventure in a more
general sense and a "free life" can thus continue to
be important:
   The gang stimulates the boy to an even greater
craving for excitement. His adolescent interest is
in that which becomes reinforced by habit; ordinary
business and pleasure seem tame and dull in
comparison with the adventure of the gang.
Habituation to this type of life in adolescence goes
a long way toward explaining behaviour in the young-
adult gangs and even of the hardened gangster.
(1927:82-83)
   The criminal who as a youngster enjoyed bumming
around talked for example about how he now at the
age of fifty-five had grown accustomed to his free
lifestyle and did not want to change it. He had
tried to live a square life but had missed the
sudden business opportunities in crime which he
still found exciting, as well as his leisure time.
Living as a criminal, he could for example go out
fishing whenever he wanted, which was his favorite
pastime.
   Addicts, of course, also get pleasure from the
adventures in their lifestyle. Sutter has formulated
this nicely when he argues against viewing addicts
from a middle-class perspective, explaining them as
double-failures, inadequate socialization, fatalism,
etc. From their own point of view - and it is
naturally their perspective which is the valid one -
their lives can be exciting, despite the mental and
physical bondage to drugs:
   Without understanding the romantic pull of the
hustling world, the colorful life of "successful"
hustlers, the sportlike challenge of the hustling
games, and the nature of the illegal marketplace, it
is impossible to grasp fully the nature of opiate

use... (1969:816)

Consequences of routinization of adventure

Adventure like everything else can reach a saturation point. Lofland refers to a "routinization of adventure" where adventure loses its quality of pleasant fear. Almost a third of the respondents stated that one of the negative features of criminal life was that it tended to get monotonous after a while. (See table 45.)

This was why some thieves had turned to drugs - to experience something new - and why some addicts who used to be on amphetamines now used heroin. A former addict:

> I used to go on uppers. The reason was due to a drug romanticism. Well, I got used to uppers and it was nothing new so then I started with brown sugar and after a while I got into shooting heroin. The reason, I guess, was to get that new exciting feeling again.

Another instance when crime stops being exciting is when the winning odds get too high, or more commonly, too low:

> It is noteworthy that... the competition may get so rough, or one party may win so much, that occasions of engagement are no longer fun or exciting. They can become merely threatening or merely fearful or merely dull, because outcomes are too highly determinate or too highly indeterminate. (Lofland, 1969:105)

The former thieves I have talked to often referred to the fact that at the end of their "careers", they got caught too easily due to their records and the time "inside" tended to increase. Finally, they saw their lives as one long prison sentence interrupted only by escapes. That was when they decided to quit.

It is interesting that their new lives as straights can also contain new experiences, thus

creating small adventures. An old ex-thief and I
went out one afternoon to buy some plants in a big
nursery. When we were in the car driving home, I
asked him what he saw as the main difference between
his former and current lives. He said that neither
one was better but the life as a thief had been fun
and exciting. But then, he added, "I never did
things like this." Doing this very straight type of
thing, going on a Sunday drive to buy plants, was a
new type of experience - a small adventure - for
him. Even making new acquaintances, getting a new
job, etc. can be a challenge, and a pleasant one if
successful:

Pleasant fear can also derive from... changes of
socal membership such as occur in getting a new job,
getting married, joining a new group or quitting any
of these. (Lofland, 1969:106)

The thief referred to above told me for example
with a certain degree of pride how he by different
means had managed to make a new start. He got a new
job for example by explaining away his lack of work
record: he told his presumptive employer that he had
had a business of his own. Thus, he managed to go
straight by thinking and planning about several such
things - something that he saw in part as a
challenge. Another example of this is the man who
stated that his big victory as an ex-addict was the
first time he was able to walk across Gustav Adolf's
Torg - a square in Malmö where addicts gather and
make their deals - without stopping.

However, if one fails to find new challenges after
switching to a square life, the boredom in the new
life might cause one to go back. Lindesmith (1947)
reports that the most common reason that ex-addicts
give for returning to drug use is boredom. In line
with this is one of the younger thieves in my study
who told me he had returned to his old criminal
friends after sitting a week in front of the
television and drinking beer, which was utterly
boring. The same attitude gave another man a reason
for divorce in order to return to his old criminal
friends:

> I'm a bit restless... I'm not really ready to get
> tied down yet (about 40 years old)... I used to
> sit home and wonder where the guys were and want
> to be out with them, drinking, sitting, shooting
> the breeze... Ya' just don't want to sit around in
> an apartment, twiddling your thumbs.

Even if one wants to quit, one might meet with
difficulties in leaving the non-routine life that
crime provides. The habit of living a shifting and
adventurous life might be hard to break. An account
of how a thief who had settled down gets into his
old life again:

> Gradually I started filling in with a group of
> fellas that were strictly thieves. I got mixed up
> with 'em just by hanging around, nothing special
> to do, inbetween jobs, filling in on a fast dollar
> here and there. After you've travelled around like
> I had and done a few things, it's pretty hard to
> settle down to a routine existence. (Martin
> 1952:48)

Being aware of the difficulty in settling down, one
interviewee even calculated a certain amount of time
for "landing" when making his plans for going
straight:

> I'm gonna start studying now and the course takes
> a good year or two and that's about what you need
> to come down again - you gotta land, get away from
> it - it's a must, otherwise you won't make it.

A last quote illustrates an attitude that is rather
typical for older criminals, when adventure has
become routine and lost its charm but the life of
the square-johns is not so appealing that one wants
to go straight. Often, in this situation, one sticks
with that which is familiar - crime. One inmate who
says he has done "everything unpleasant" (with a
laughter) - living with a prostitute, smuggling

drugs and liquor, among other things - makes the
following reflection about his life:

"You're so screwed up you don't know what to
choose. Instead you try everything to see what it
can give you."
"You're sort of chasing something?"
"Yeah, I guess so. We who're here have seen so
much shit. We've done **too many** things... And after
a while you get so tired of everything, the
society and all, there's nothing that interests
you. I guess one would like to have a job and a
steady income but it's sort of a drag to get
there..."
"It's not enough?"
"Well, maybe it would be but we don't have that
routine... on the other hand, those who're in it
might feel bad about it, but what in hell are they
to do? They're stuck with loans, taxes and shit.
So for them it's just a matter of clinging to what
they've got."
"Are you better off in that way?"
"Yeah, I don't **owe** anyone anything. But that's not
good or bad, maybe it's actually what's
lacking..."
"Not having any commitments?"
"Yeah, nothing that directs you."

Secrecy

Secrecy in itself can have positive functions for
individuals as well as for groups. For the
individual it can provide a clearer identity based
on a belonging to a special group. Furthermore,
secrecy can give him or her a feeling that he
experiences something **more** and something **else** than
most people:
    ... the secret produces an immense enlargement of
life:... The secret offers, so to speak, the
possibility of a second world alongside the manifest
world; and the latter is decisively influenced by
the former. (Simmel, 1964:330)

Secondly, secrecy has positive functions for a group. It can strengthen its ties, as well as give the group members a feeling of exclusiveness. The mere using of a forbidden drug can accomplish this:

No substance was more profoundly tabooed by conventional middle-class society. Regular heroin use provides a sense of maximal social differentiation from the "square". (Finestone, 1969:792)

Here, however, I will mainly discuss the social-psychological aspects of secrecy for the individual involved with criminality. A general fascination with secrecy seemed to exist among the interviewees. A former thief:

Inside there's a lot of criminal bullshitting about different plans what you're going to do when you get out... schemes and stuff they give each other. But it's all lies, all of it. It's just to have something to talk about... Plans and drafts that they hide or set on fire so that no one will find the... Or codes so that the bulls won't find them. In other words, it's sort of **mysterious** things.

When one reveals something a bit sensitive, or secrets about one's personal life, one tends to whisper or lower one's voice. This behavior was quite usual during the interviews. When my respondents talked about drugs or different methods in selling stolen goods, for example, they seemed to feel that they revealed something, almost like a gift - a confidence of this kind is something, as Simmel has pointed out, that cannot be requested: it is given.

One reason for this fascination for secrecy can be as McKenzie has noted about secret groups in general, that they have an identity-solving function for people who have felt they had few bonds with society as a whole or lacked close ties to other groups:

The individual who formerly felt exposed and

vulnerable is likely to find that membership in such a group gives him reassurance to the outer world. Though he may continue to live and work in that world, he no longer depends on it in the same way. He is able to withdraw from it, and to find the reciprocal confidence on which the existence of the secret society depends. This new sense of fellowship may create such powerful bonds that the member feels invulnerable to the outside world. (1967:251)

Coleman, who writes about addicts, notes that labelling oneself as such can actually be described as an identity gain. He gives this quote as an illustration:

> I never labelled myself as anything. Now I was labelling myself as a doper. And there was a certain mystique about the whole dope culture. It set you apart and I labelled that as being something special. I liked to think of myself as being the vanguard of society. I felt I was the wave of the future and that everybody would be smoking eventually. (1975:115)

It is interesting, in this context, to note Blumer et al.'s (1967) observation - contrary to the common belief - that addicts seldom try to convert others into drug use. This can be interpreted as due to the fact that they want to retain the feeling of being an exclusive group. Belonging to such a group gives the members possession of "inside secrets". "Being in the know" can in itself give a feeling of superiority due to the exclusive knowledge of, say, how to open a safe or how to use different drugs. Finestone's comment on the heroin user's world:

It is the restricted extent of the distribution of drug use, the scheming and intrigue associated with underground "connections" through which drugs are obtained, the secret lore of the appreciation of the drug's effects, which give the cat the exhilaration of participating in a conspiracy. (1969:798)

Another type of secret as Goffman (1959) notes, is the "strategic", a secret which is used as a lever

against another group in order to prevent them from
hindering one's planned actions. Secrets of this
type were for example ways of smuggling drugs into
prison. One strategy here was blackmailing guards
into smuggling for the inmates. Blackmail was
possible because the inmates had seen guards
stealing food, clothes, etc. Through this secret
knowledge, the inmates seemed to derive a feeling of
revenge towards the system as well as a sense of
power. A former addict whom I spoke to was rather
upset with the guards who did things like this. He
was now working with rehabilitation and therefore
visited prisons where he had formerly been an inmate
himself. Sometimes he saw guards there who had
smuggled drugs for him - due to his blackmailing
them. With the self-righteousness of the former
addict, he said that he had been thinking of
revealing what they had done, because their actions
had been wrong, even though he did not think they
had continuted with their smuggling. But he had
decided that since they had families, he would not
do it. The knowledge he possessed however gave him a
sense of power, which he seemed to enjoy.
   Other positive strategic secrets are seen in
situations where a thief sells to buyers who are not
sure of his identity. It gives the thief a feeling
of being the one who is in control. A man commenting
on selling stolen goods to workers at a factory,
whom he got to know quite well, but:

   "You can't tell 'em too much 'cause then they
   might get greedy and that's no good... They
   probably don't know who I am, then they might've
   had another attitude. But we've had a good time. I
   guess they look at me as the guy who can fix
   things, so they might believe I'm just doing it
   for their sake, I don't know." (laughter)
   "Santa Claus?"
   "Right!"

It is interesting that the opposite situation,
knowing that others know but that they cannot take

action, can also evoke the same feeling of being the one who is in control. This is, for example, the case when the police know about crimes that are committed, but do not have evidence against the criminal. A few respondents said things like "the police knew about it, but they couldn't do anything, you see". Letkemann (1973) notes that the criminal who sees himself as experienced, i.e., not an amateur, was more concerned about conviction than detection. As long as the police "had nothing on him it didn't matter". The fact that others know, but cannot do anything, can be seen as part of the challenge. To outwit the police in a conscious way is of course more thrilling than to just get away with it with no feed-back - especially since the police are one of the significant audiences for criminals.

Finally one can assume that the mystique and secretness surrounding the criminal life can be beneficial for those who quit and know how to put their former identity to good use:

There is ... a sympathy bestowed upon the ex-addict that is not unlike that given to the reclaimed sinner who has changed his way and come back to the fold of society. Add to this an element of the glamor that attaches itself to men (not women) who have countered society's morals and laws, and one finds a certain mystique bestowed upon the ex-addict. (Waldorf, 1973:26)

The fact that some ex-criminals partly support themselves through lectures in schools and elsewhere, about their former life, and that biographies and auto-biographies by criminals seem to be such a lucrative business, might be explained by the fact that the secretness in itself is something attractive:

From secrecy, which shades all that is profound and significant, grows the typical error according to which everything mysterious is something important and essential. Before the unknown, man's natural impulse to idealize and his natural fearfulness cooperate toward the same goal: to enter

the unknown through imagination, and to pay
attention to it with an emphasis that is not
usually accorded to patent reality. (Simmel,
1964:333)

Independence

The importance of independence and individualism for
criminals has been a reoccurring theme in this book.
Since it can be seen as a reward and a value in
itself and something which many intervieews stated
that they achieved through being criminals it will
be further discussed here. The prospect of losing
one's independence was seen as a problem if one
planned to quit criminality. The quote below from a
young thief who wanted to support himself legally in
the future is an example of how he might get into
trouble doing this:

"It's important with individualism?"
"That's the most important thing... if there's no
place for that I don't wanna join the game... It's
that, I guess, that's made me... that's the reason
I don't function in a society like this. Not in
any society where I'm just a member of a flock,
because I want to develop myself. I only live once
and it's my life and I can't put that into the
hands of some big collective that won't give
anything back... just because that's the way it's
supposed to be."

Chic Conwell, the thief in Sutherland's *The
Professional Thief* even attributes the problem in
quitting crime to the dependence this implies:
   To steal a living is strictly an individual
affair, in which he is not dependent upon anyone
else except, perhaps, some partners. But he cannot
be independent when he tries to quit stealing.
(1958:188)
   To work as a criminal can thus be seen as part of
the claimed independence. Another part is probably
their marginal situation, discussed elsewhere in

this work. This marginality breeds a feeling of individuality and independence from ways of living that others take for granted or follow unconsciously:

Actually, what we are prone to call 'individualism' is not so much anything that may be seen to emerge from the individual, considered as a discrete entity, but, rather, from the individual's relation to a considerable number of groups or other types of social aggregates. His power of thought, imagination, and action may be heightened by the experience of living at one and the same time on the peripheries of many groups, as well as values and themes. Not one but several social groups may be his reference groups. (Nisbet, 1970:110)

Areas of independence

Even if many respondents stated that it was important to be independent, this was expressed with varying degrees of clarity as to what was important in independence.[9] Some meant, for example, that they were more independent than most people concerning **general laws, rules of behavior**, etc.

"What is important about independence?"
"That's difficult - you can be independent just up to a certain limit. But, of course, we can be much more independent than normal people. They are so dependent on so many other things, like how society is regulated, and following certain norms. We aren't to the same extent."

The inmates often stated that they wanted to remain free from time-schedules, installment plans, laws, etc. - to avoid regulations that are forced on one by external sources:

There're so many rules around you - I guess we were just born different than most people. You just can't take that other type of life (the

squares) because you'll be a prisoner in that life
as well with a lot of installments and nothing
left, so you have to live like a robot... You can
never choose for yourself, the guard out here, he
can't choose his life, he can't leave tomorrow and
be away for ten days. Even if he's a bachelor,
everything would just break down if he did
something like that. So you want to be independent
of everything. Of course we have to have laws and
I'm prepared to follow them up to a certain extent
but then I want something in exchange as well, not
only misery.

In relation to **work** they saw an ordinary job (often
equated with a factory job) as negative, implying a
loss of freedom. It is important to note that it is
not work in itself but the situation around work
that seems to generate a feeling of subordination.

"It's difficult... I think everybody here has
difficulties in subordinating himself to any sort
of routine or regulated existence. They really
dislike anyone who's screaming at them at a job. I
would like to see any inmate here who would go to
work at a factory. (laughter)

Even the idea of having to make excuses for sick
leaves can imply a humiliation:

But living with square-johns is different. If I
don't want to work tonight I don't see any reason
why I have to go into a detailed explanation with
the official out there. I just say that I don't
feel like working and I lay off. But a square-john
wants to get real complicated and have their wife
call up and say that they are sick. You are much
more your own boss when you are working as a
thief. All thieves hate regimentation which is
something they have to accept when they go to a
penitentiary. (Chambliss and King, 1972: 157)

Thus, when asked why they reject work, the answers

were not usually based on reasons such as that the jobs available were low-paid, low-status, etc., but centered rather on the routine of a job and the demand of applying oneself continuously. Finestone's comment on heroinists fits well with my repondent's attitudes:

The self-constraint required by work was construed as an unwarranted damper upon his love for spontaneity. The other undesirable element from his point of view was the authoritarian setting of most types of work with which he was familiar. (1969:793)

Finestone's interpretation of the above is that of devices for sustaining "the cat's" self-conception. "The cat's feeling of superiority would be openly challenged, were he to confront certain of the social realities of his situation..." (ibid). These social realities are discrimination and the types of low-status jobs that are the only ones available, and independence from these is a basic requirement that the "cats" have.

Not only a particular self-image at a given time is important, but also previous experiences. Having been under other people's supervision, such as in orphanages or prison, can of course influence a wish to decide for oneself in a work situation:

I've had a whole lot of jobs, but I've never felt good there - there's always been someone over me making the decisions. It's been that way ever since I was a kid (he had been in orphanages since he was two years old). That means that now if someone at work wants to order me about, I do the opposite. I mean, I want to decide for myself.

The subordination they see in ordinary jobs is thus connected with a feeling of lack of **respect** connected with these jobs. This is closely correlated to what type of job one can accept in the legal market:
... the **thief** sometimes "reforms" and tries to succeed in some life within the law. Such behavior, contrary to popular notions, is quite acceptable to

other members of the thief subculture, so long as the new job and position are not "anti-criminal" and do not involve regular, routine "slave labor". (Sutherland and Cressey, 1978:612)

Thus as long as these jobs are not defined as 'slave jobs', legitimate work can be accepted and even desired, if it contains 'respect':

> But you can't change people like us. That's wrong to say that. I don't know - if I could get out and get me a good job, if there was some respect went with it... I'm not going to get out and work in a service station or work in a drive-in grocery store or sell peanuts or something like that. I'm just not going to do it. I've had some good jobs in my life, but I could never get one again. I'm getting old now... I've got to get out and make me some money. Try to get in business for myself. (Jackson, 1969:235)

The connection of independence and **time** has been discussed elsewhere in this work but since this is an important and often-mentioned aspect, a few words here as well are in keeping.

One of the objections in having a nine-to-five job was just that: nine to five, confining one during that time-span. Three out of four inmates thus wanted to have free working hours. The inmates even considered free working hours as something self-evident, a must. However, fixed times and routines, as we know, structure and order the day. In a study of mine (Persson, 1980) among ordinary people, many expressed mixed feelings toward free working hours. In one way they saw it as preferable, but on the other hand felt it left too much to one's own initiative to "get up and go". Thinking about being a salesman instead of working at a butcher shop as he did, one of those "ordinary men" made the following reflection which I think is a quite common one for most people who are used to regulated times:

> I'm afraid I would postpone the things I had to do

and then be stuck with them later... It would be nice to take off some afternoons, you can do that, in that job, but at the same time I would have a bad conscience - and no one would be around... And it's nice the way I have it now, when I'm free, I'm free... and I always know when I'm at work and when I'm not.

That criminals do not want to subordinate themselves to time regulations is sometimes even expressed in not wanting to wait in queues. This can even lead some to steal in stores - even if this was not planned - instead of having to wait in line. This attitude is also connected to the self-evident attitude towards owning and driving a car, regardless of whether one has a driver's licence or not. When I asked one of the respondents what he needed when he got out, he said "a car". When I asked why, he replied that there was no way he would use "peoplemobiles" (city buses). The degrading tone in the slang word expresses somewhat his attitude and enhances his explanation that he could not stand the waiting and queuing involved in using public transportation.

Most of the inmates wanted to have a steady relationship with a woman and saw this as an important factor in "getting their lives together". At the same time they did not wish to be too "tied down", i.e. they shrived for independence in their **relationships.**

In the questionnaire given to inmates and to the control group, the question in table 50 reflects the inmates' special attitude.

The result is interesting especially in the discrepancy between traditional thieves and white-collar workers, which I think reflects basic differences in values: very traditional ones as opposed to more modern ones, as well as in different requirements for independence.

Quite a few of the thieves liked it if their wife or woman did not work. They, on the other hand, wanted to be able to tend to business outside the

Table 50.   "Even if I live with a woman I want to
be able to come and go as I please,
without always having to tell her
where I am going and when I am coming
back."

%	Agree	Disagree	No opinion	Sum	N
All inmates	52	28	20	100	(116)
Thereof traditional					
thieves	62	24	14	100	(37)
Blue-collar					
workers	28	54	18	100	(105)
White-collar					
workers	18	69	13	100	(93)

home without having to answer to her. An attitude of
"minding your own business" in a relationship was
also seen as practical. As some pointed out, if you
do not tell your wife your whereabouts and your
business, she is not in a position to tell the
police. "What she doesn't know, won't hurt her. Or
me."

Most of the respondents emphasized that they kept
their distance to most people. Some called
themselves "lone wolves" and this was not a negative
epithet, rather, the contrary. They said this with a
certain pride and pointed out that they acted
according to their own wishes. Social distance is
however not only a matter of preference. Their
lifestyle in itself creates distances: they realize
that they might have to pay a psychological or
emotional price for becoming too attached to people,
since they are aware of the fact that they might
soon have to part due to a new prison sentence or to
the general uncertainty and instability of their
lives. An ex-thief said for example that his
relationship with his daughter had become much
closer because nowadays they could make plans for
the future. Earlier, he could not afford to get too
fond of her due to the ever-present possibility of
arrest.

Most criminals also want to be independent from criminal **organisations**:

Popular notions not withstanding, the basic units of a heistmob are not a 'mastermind' and some servile morons who carry out his orders. As a matter of fact, among 'heavy' thieves no one gives orders for the good reason that no one takes them - the heavy is as independent a character as walks the earth. (DeBaun, 1950:72)

The self-respecting thieves in my study also rejected involvement with associates who ordered them around. King, the thief whom Chambliss wrote a biography about, had the same view of not letting any criminal organization make his decisions and he even stole from "the syndicate" - something he derived an obvious satisfaction from:

> If I went to an Eastern state, Id beat the syndicate (steal from the syndicate's bars)... And I thought it was a big joke - it never did come out in the papers, you know, naturally, but that syndicate went crazy. I guess they tore half of the hoods up in Cincinatti trying to find out who did it. We did from out here. Cause we had no fear, no respect for the syndicates - heck with them, you know. (Chambliss and King, 1982:28-29)

Thieves did not like addicts for many reasons, but one of their main objections toward the addicts was that in drug circles, those who had drugs were seen as "kings" and those below in the hierarchy degraded themselves by flattery and letting themselves be used in different ways in order to get drugs.

Most thieves seem to have a definite view concerning **drug use** vis-a-vis dependency. To become a slave to a drug is as bad as being dependent on anything else. This might explain the contempt which one of the self-righteous criminals, for whom independence was one of the most important things in life (he proudly stated that he was independent of everyone in the legal as well as the illegal world), had for addicts and pushers inside prison:

"Those who run around here selling drugs, they're clowns, they're bums, they're bastards... They're trying to create some kind of big-shot atmosphere inside prison for a few grams of amphetamine. It's shit, to put it plainly."
"Do you feel sorry for the addicts?"
"No, they're the same kind of trash, so... If you want to use, you should be able to hold it inside yourself and keep it your own business. And in that case, people shouldn't touch you. If I bring in my own stuff and don't hurt anyone, then that's my business..."

So, the traditional thieves try to maintain a certain **dignity**, which, as Lukes has pointed out, is a value intrinsic in the concept of individualism. Many spoke with disdain about the rushing around that occurred in prison and the begging of money when drugs had been smuggled in. "They don't act like human beings..."

Independence as a necessity

Freedom or independence can have a practical function for criminals. Independence from commitments to jobs, in relationships, time-schedules, etc. allows his activity as a criminal to be optimal.
   Even owning things was sometimes perceived as a commitment that could tie one down. Subsequently, some of the respondents felt that they did not want to own a new car, a boat, etc. because if they did, they would have to take care of them - something that was difficult to do within the frame of their lifestyle and with the possibility or prospect of being arrested always hanging overhead. One of the interviewees said, for example, that he always rented cars, boats, and apartments instead of buying these things because he did not want to be "tied down".
   Liebow, who has written about black street-corner

men, sees their situation as discouraging commitment:

Thus, the constant awareness of a future loaded with "trouble" results in a constant readiness to leave, to "make it", to "get out of town", and discourages the man from sinking roots into the world he lives in... it discourages him from committing himself to a job, expecially one whose payoffs lies in the promise of a future reward rather than in the present. In the same way, it discourages him from deep and lasting commitments to family and friends or to any other persons, places or things, since such commitments could hold him hostage, limiting his freedom of movement and thereby compromising his security which lies in that freedom. (1967: 70-71)

Several studies of other groups in insecure positions, e.g., Howell's *Hard Living on Clay Street*, Anderson's *The Hobo*, and Milners' *Black Players* show the same attitude towards independence. It might be that people who are in these situations "make a virtue of necessity". This might be one reason why independence achieves a value of its own.

Independence for its own sake

Writing about personal autonomy, Shibutani notes:

The expression of one's individuality - the preservation of those distinctive habits of thought and action which characterize a man and mark him off from all others - may itself become a value. (1961:307)

In a world where formal merits are lacking and do not count very highly, one's personality and autonomy seem to achieve a special value of their own. Among the respondents, "integrity" for example was a generally valued trait. In prison this might become even more important:

Once a man has gone through the impersonal procedures necessary to processing and labeling him as a criminal and a prisoner, about all he has left in the world is his "self". No matter what that self may be, he takes elaborate steps to protect it, to guard it, to maintain it. If it should be taken away from him, even in the name of rehabilitation or treatment, he will have lost everything. (Sutherland and Cressey, 1978:558)

A young thief in my study, who explained his criminality by his wish for freedom, even claimed he was free to a certain degree in prison, since he could still protect his "self": they did not lock up his thoughts:

> "If you've ever experienced freedom you won't let anyone catch you a second time... you look for it everywhere. I sought it in an intense criminality, that was one way, 'cause then, nobody could make demands on me or rule me. But later on, it unfortunately got me to prison and here you're pretty locked up." (laughter)
> "Yeah."
> "Yeah... but on the other hand it's only the body they lock in, it's not your... thoughts..."

As a final comment, I think that the craving for independence found among criminals is a particularly interesting facet in that they both believe in and seek independence while at the same time must live by strict rules and constraints. One can question whether there really is less conformity among criminals. Due to several factors such as being in prison and needing contacts in their work, they are in many ways very dependent on people and circumstances. This should lead to a greater social control.

It is a small world and one's reputation seems to be long-lived. There are few escapes from the label "ratter" for example. One former thief and addict who presently works in a treatment center for addicts claims for example that his reputation of having been a "right guy" helps him in his present job. If he had been known as a "ratter" he believes that he would not have made it.

The independence claimed by the respondents, then,

might reflect more a value or cultural norm than the reality of most criminals. The criminal world seems full of rules and norms circumscribing independence. There are rules about being generous, rules about drug taking, norms about honor among thieves, etc. Yet although a lot of time is spent in prison - the destructive effect this total institution has on individuality has been thoroughly explained by Goffman (1961) - criminality is still defined as independence: this is one of the fascinating inherent contradictions in the criminal lifestyle which has not been resolved in this study, but has at least been observed and described.

SUMMARY

Several scholars have written about crime as work
and have perhaps over-emphasized the professionalism
involved in being a thief or a drug dealer. Most of
the interviewed persons in this study had had
ordinary legal jobs as well as illegal ones. They
tended to view crime both as work and non-work,
i.e., crime is usually not seen as an occupation **per
se.**

The inmates stated however certain necessary
prerequisites if one were to be able to support
oneself through crime: the importance of having
"nerve" and of "keeping one's cool" in stressful
situations for example. These skills were more
important than craftmanship in crime. They also
stated that crime as work was a very arduous way of
making money. One interesting and neglected feature
involved is the need to actively acquire knowledge
and the necessary creativity; I say neglected
because so much emphasis has been placed on a
tutelage process, that people think learning crime
is easy. According to my respondents, learning
through older or more experienced criminals was not
enough: they had to rely a great deal as well on
their own initiative and ideas in order to make
contacts, to think up new crimes, etc. It is
important to be aware of this active use of

ingenuity and knowledge in order to understand the pride felt by many of the criminals. It is also important, I think, to appreciate that knowledge of crime, as any other type of knowledge, can be viewed as an investment from the actor's point of view.

To lead a criminal life involves beating the system not only in connection with criminal activities. Certain strategies are therefore developed in order to keep a front vis-a-vis the police, social workers, etc. These strategies can be seen as both instrumental and symbolic. The first is exemplified in cases such as using one's criminal identity in order to take advantage of prisoner organizations or to stay unemployed, or by referring to one's past if there is a risk of being given a job. There are also strategies for manipulating different rehabilitation efforts by officials. The symbolic value of beating the system is seen in its giving a sense of control over one's own life.

Crime is seen not only as a kind of work, it is also defined by many criminals as business. To be a thief was for example often referred to as "being one's own boss". Crime actually shares some of the characteristics of the legal business world. Thieves need, for example, to know the demands of the market and drug dealers must have some 'seed money'. Furthermore, many of the respondents claimed that one could work oneself up in a world of rough competition. The respondents did not dream about a mafia type of organized business, however. They preferred their "business" to be small and manageable, which allowed them to remain independent and keep control. Many criminals thus see themselves as businessmen and they also want - when and if they are going straight - to have a business type of occupation. They were in fact more positive to having a business of their own than the control group representing ordinary people. The inmates had also owned small businesses to a larger extent than had the comparison sample. The wish to have a business and the tendency of criminals to look at themselves as businessmen were explained by their wanting to remain free from the constraints of 9-to-5 jobs, which the interviewees looked very negatively upon. Furthermore, it seemed as if the special type of businessman they wanted to be was the one who lived an action-filled life where fast decisions and sudden wealth were the motivations. Action **per se** seemed to be a gratification, rather than acquiring status and success in society in general, as the innovators that Merton portrayed.

Criminals have often been described as using different techniques for denial of responsibility. I found, however, that thieves to a higher degree than the control group stated that it was one's own fault if one became a criminal. The control group on the other hand placed greater emphasis on upbringing in explaining why someone becomes a criminal. It seems as if ordinary people have learned to apply the kind of sociological and psychological explanations of criminality available through the mass media.

Thieves do not only claim individual responsibility concerning why they themselves have been criminals but they also seem to have a general negative attitude towards determinism. Few agreed, for example, to the statement "Once a thief, always a thief". All inmates - also addicts - believed furthermore that it is up to the individual if he is to quit crime or drugs. This is, as I see it, not only due to a value-based individualism but is partly a realistic attitude. An unshakable determinism to go straight is, perhaps, necessary if they are to succeed in the struggle of changing their lives. They often lack safety-nets, family, education, work experience, etc. as help along the way when they try to leave criminality. It is in fact to a large degree up to them themselves if they will make it as lawful citizens. The thieves also thought that they should take the consequences of their criminality. They stated, for example, that it was their own fault if they got caught; it was not due to bad company or the skills of the police as much as to their own clumsiness, lack of planning, etc. The same tendency to take the consequences is seen in the readiness that many showed for accepting prison sentences as a price for one's criminality.

Two things seem to be connected to this sense of individualistic responsibility among thieves. They claim that once you are a grown-up, you are and should be able to make your own decisions and take the consequences for your choices. Secondly, thieves often have old-fashioned ideals of manliness. This is evident for example in that they more often than the control group think that it is the man who should support the family.

As I see it, there are three possible reasons for this individualistic morality among thieves. The first is that it is functional for the group if the individual takes the blame upon himself. The second is that they tend to see themselves as the action-seekers that Goffman has described. Doing this implies a view of oneself as voluntarily choosing, taking responsibility for one's actions and showing "character" in case ones projects fail. The third is that criminals can be seen as "marginal men", i.e., having lived and identified themselves with several cultures. For people in marginal positions, choices are not uncomplicated but need to be thought through and weighed and are therefore more conscious than the choices of those who live in more "taken-for-granted" worlds, which produces a rather existentialistic attitude towards one's own actions.

Criminologists have often considered criminals as being oriented to the present. In my opinion, this view gives a simplified and partially misleading picture. Because of the nature of the criminal world, criminals are forced to make fast decisions, vital for their future. Furthermore, "hanging around" is necessary in order for them take advantage of opportunities that may suddenly arise. Criminals often demand more independence than most other groups and thus more manipulative time for themselves. This special kind of constant orientation to the future is probably in general more common among groups that lead an irregular, unpredictable life.

I have tried to reverse somewhat the view of criminals as denying responsibility and as hedonistically present-oriented. There is yet another belief about criminals that has been criticized here, namely that of their being socially unskilled. Not only con men but thieves, addicts, prostitutes, etc. need social skills in order for example to make an identification of other crooks, customers, undercover police, and so on. To do this they have to learn to size up people, develop a sense of whom to trust. Furthermore, they need to hide their own identity in some situations. This forces them to develop skills in "passing" and "appearing normal". Criminals are also more dependent on contacts than on formal merits, which leads to skills in managing people. Yet another reason for socal skills is their marginal position. They have lived in different worlds and are therefore quite aware of differences between people in values, behavior, etc.

The attainment of money was a common explanation among the respondents as to why they lead a criminal life. Money is viewed in a slightly different way than by the control group, however. Firstly, many of the criminals stated that they wanted only "enough" to get by with - but this could mean quite a lot if one compared it with most people's spending abilities. Inmates also described themselves as spendthrifts. They stated that money did not, and should not, mean a lot. They looked down on those who could not see money as a medium purely for buying things and they argued that money should be used, not kept or saved. At the same time those criminals who had money were viewed with respect. Furthermore, big spending seemed to be used as a means to show off. Simmel's article, *The Miser and the Spendthrift*, is helpful in explaining this somewhat contradictory way of looking at money, i.e., that it supposedly does not matter while at the same time it has great importance. Since criminals described themselves as spendthrifts, I was surprised by the repetitive talk about the subject of money. Simmel argues however that spendthrifts are really as interested in money as the miser: it is just hidden under a man-of-the-world attitude. The fascination with money is expressed in the spending itself; i.e., the interest is not placed on the objects acquired.

The respondents often compared themselves with the squares. The reason for this was that this latter lifestyle was seen as the alternative to the criminal one. The only advantage in the lifestyle of the squares that the majority of inmates agreed on was the absence of time spent in prison. The main criticism against the square's lifestyle was that it was considered boring. Conventional people were furthermore looked upon as being naive, as imprisoned by society's rules and regulations, having bad finances and being envious. It is interesting that this view has its counterpart in the opinion many other groups, such as intellectuals, "professional debaters", etc., have of common people. The inmates did not seem to be bitter or hostile towards the squares however, as is sometimes assumed. Instead they seemed to have a condescending attitude towards them, which was reflected in the fact that many thought they were "okay" but added things like "amazing that they can stand it" or "society can't make it without them". This rather detached attitude was not totally uncomplicated however. The respondents had lived a lawful life at times, associated with conventional people and thus knew personally of the problems concerning understanding between themselves and the squares. These difficulties arose primarily from a difference in experiences which could make for uneasiness both in understanding in a general sense as well as in simple conversation. The experiences that criminals had were, however, said to be more "real" and interesting than those of the squares. This also seems to have a societal background in that we interpret "experiences" as something that is connected with things of an unusual or odd character.

The negative view towards the squares' lifestyle made most respondents state that if they went straight, they would find a way to support themselves legally but not live like the squares. What was meant by this "third alternative", however, seemed hard to define. Maybe this difficulty in picturing something different from a criminal or a square lifestyle is one of the reasons why it seems so problematic to "go legal".

When I began to interview inmates, I was struck by the emphasis placed on the positive sides of a criminal life. Due to this as well as the more common reports of the dull and depressing facts of their situation, I decided to pay specific interest to the "rewards" of crime. Some of these attractions are pretty obvious, such as the economic aspect. At least within a limited time perspective, crime can be lucrative. Since criminals can be described as action-seekers, the exciting, adventurous features of illegalities are obviously a rewarding factor. A less evident attraction in a criminal lifestyle is its secrecy, which in itself gives it an air of fascination. Finally, independence is discussed since this so often was stated as important by the interviewees and thus given a value of its own. Freedom could be found in a criminal life through avoiding rules and regulations in society and by having free work hours. There seemed to be a higher general demand for independence. Even in relationships with women, thieves wanted to be able to come and go as they wished. In this respect they differed quite a lot from the control group.

The real freedom seekers among the thieves also emphasized that one should remain independent from criminal organizations as well as from drugs. It is interesting that this high demand for independence and search for freedom is so accentuated in a group – criminality as such is sometimes explained as a wish for independence – which in many ways is so restricted. Someone, for example, took up the contradiction in his life – that he was sitting in prison although he was describing himself as a freedom-seeker, but said that even if he was locked up, no one could take his thoughts away. In this sense independence as such acquires a value of its own. Not only prison however limits the individuality among this group. It is such a small group, so special, and relying so much on informal communication that the social control and pressure might be greater than in many other groups. This should of course have a strong moderating influence on independent actions and thoughts. These somehow contradictory facts about criminals - their craving for freedom and stating that they are more independent than other groups while at the same time being severely limited in these respects - are however one of the things that makes this group so interesting to study.

NOTES

Introduction

1. E.g. Maurer (1962), Shover (1971).
2. Sutherland (1937), Shover (1971), Letkemann (1973), West (1974), Polsky (1969).
3. Zetterberg (1977) defines the concept as a number of related actions that the practioners have in common and which they find particularly engaging.
4. See Matza (1967) for a critique of subcultural analysis often being too deterministic.
5. Apart from my own results, see for example Glaser (1964).

Chapter 1

1. Cf. Mack (1972).

Chapter 2

1. For a critique of general criminological causality research, see Walker (1977) *Behavior and Misbehavior*.
2. For similar conclusions, see Irwin (1980) and Shover (1971).
3. Cf. Miller (1978) and Gould (1968).

4. Shover (1971) equated burglary skills with skilled manual trades. Gould (1968) however notes that crime today is at best a semi-skilled occupation.
5. The other alternatives were mentioned in the following order: "Someone who helps others" (31 %), "Someone who lives like the squares but supports himself through criminality" (25 %), "Someone who is sharp and keeps his head, who sees through society" (24 %), "Someone who is skilful in supporting himself through stealing, robbery, fencing, etc. (someone who always has money)" (17 %), "Someone who has a lot of drugs" (14 %), "Someone who carries off clever, bold jobs and dares to take chances" (14 %), "One who keeps to himself and manages by himself" (13 %), "Someone who is tough and does not give in to other people" (8 %), "One who's not afraid to open his trap, who can jive (trick or convince others so that he himself gains)" (6 %), "Someone who does crazy things and doesn't care about conventions, who 'does his own thing'" (5 %).
6. Klockars reports that the fence he studied engaged in similar practices.
7. See Sellerberg (1982) for the importance of these institutions in creating trust in modern transactions.

Chapter 3

1. See Goffman (1961) for numerous examples from life in mental hospitals, and Crozier and Friedberg (1980) on the importance of beating the system from the actor's point of view in extending his 'margin of liberty'.
2. See Sutherland (1937). Nor is this reserved for what Cressey (1972) has called "persistent criminals" or Shover (1971) "good burglars".
3. Aubert (1979:11-13).

Chapter 4.

1. The percentage is highest for the traditional thieves, 32 %, and lowest for the mixed category, 15 %, for having had a legal business.
2. Cf. Tham (1979: 130), where he shows that 9.4 % of all those cited in official records (i.e. including those cited for minor offences) have had or have a small business, as compared to 6.9 % of the total population in Sweden.
3. The sum of money given to each inmate upon release, to help him get on his feet.
4. Cf. Miller (1958), Prus and Irini (1980).
5. Cf. Adler and Adler (1980) for drug dealers and the conflict of keeping their business secret and at the same time wanting to show off successful dealing by, for example, being involved in "the fast life".

Chapter 5.

1. Cf. Shover (1971).
2. In the foreword of Parker and Allerton (1962).
3. Cf. Shover (1971).
4. The classic account of the concept is Goffman's *Stigma* (1961).
5. Bondeson (1974).
6. For more of this type of description of addicts as non-retreatists, see Sutter (1969, 1972), Preble (1969) and Proctor (1971).
7. Cf. Shover (1971) who compares "the good burglar" he studied with gamblers, Prus and Irini (1980) see action as one part of "rounding as a way of life". (Rounder = thief or hustler). See also Taylor (1984) for the same attitude amongst professional criminals in Britain.
8. It can be noted that Miller's (1958) thesis of the lower-class' culture as emphasizing fate is not given any total support here.
9. For a theoretical statement on this, see Lofland (1969) and for empirical results, see West (1974).

10. For similar results, see Glaser (1964: 475).
11. Holzman (1979) has described the burglars and robbers he studied as moonshining in crime, since crime was their secondary income rather than their first.
12. See also Taylor (1984) where the professional criminals he studied claim that the same is true in England.
13. I am not arguing that ratting does not occur, only that the norm against it is at least restrictive.
14. The more common interpretation of this norm in prison research is that it serves to keep the inmate power system in line and to protect the leaders.

Chapter 6.

1. Many scholars, e.g. Corrigan (1976), Hannerz (1969) and Whyte (1943), have written about the socializing aspect of hanging out on street corners, etc. Though this is an important aspect, especially for the learning of criminal knowledge, this article deals mainly with the practical aspects of 'hanging out', thus being available for any opportunities and for strategic people (such as customers, fences, etc.).
2. There are naturally different ways of waiting and making oneself accessible. The availability of the established fence can be compared to that of a veterinary surgeon or doctor on duty. The fence described by Klockars had, however, even succeeded in minimizing this aspect of work:
   "Three years ago, when he was younger and healthier, thieves and drivers would come by at all hours with merchandise... I've stopped that bullshit now, but a couple a years ago it was murder. Twelve, one, two, three o'clock in the morning the door bell would ring. I cut the bell wire and they'd bang on the door and throw pebbles up at my window. That's the business. It

never stops." (1974: 72)

3. Hall (1959) and deGrazia (1964) designate this
    type of time-use as "linear-mechanistic".
    Perhaps the relevant sociological concept of a
    time-perspective among criminals would be that
    of a 'cyclic perspective'. This term has been
    applied by Calkins when describing patients as a
    mental hospital: "...in this perspective time
    moves in a cyclic fashion from turning point to
    turning point or from crisis to crisis... The
    points comprise high-lights of experience as
    defined by the actor. Time is fragmented and
    chaotic as compared to the orderly continuum of
    the precise mechanistic perspective." (1970:
    490).

Chapter 7.

1. Cf. Goffman's (1966) concept of "cognitive
    recognition".
2. Sarnecki, 1982.
3. See Stonequist (1937:184-200) about how light
    blacks passed as whites.
4. In Bondeson's (1974) study of Swedish prisoners,
    as many as 69 % of the inmates answered that
    they believed that "few" or "no one" could see
    or otherwise tell that an individual had been in
    prison, which argues against the belief that the
    stigmatizing of a prison stay is so deep that
    others can actually spot it by just looking at a
    former inmate.
5. Komarovsky (1947).
6. Lofland (1976: 55) has also pointed out that
    underdogs will develop a self with a dramaturgic
    quality since the powerful by definition can
    punish or reward them. They thus develop a
    consciousness of how they can manipulate others.
7. See Piliavian and Briar (1964), Cicourel (1976).
8. Goffman (1959:35)
9. The bar he describes was actually studied by
    Roebuck and Frese, *The Rendezvous*, Free Press,
    New York, (1976).

10. Cf. McIntosh (1971) and Gould (1968).
11. Cf. Goffmans book *Stigma* (1961).

Chapter 8.

1. An illustration of the need for "ordinary
   people" to plan their budget as opposed to the
   lack of this need among criminals is reflected,
   I think, in this result:

"Before I go out shopping, I make a shoppinglist."

%	Agree	Disagree	No opinion	Sum	N
All inmates	21	64	15	100	(127)
SIFO	58	33	9	100	(125)

2. Cf. Taylor et al. (1973).

Chapter 9.

1. Kelly (1966) from an unpublished manuscript
   quoted in Bannister and Mair (1968: 45).
2. For a critique of the reality behind this
   commonly held view, see Whyte (1956) and
   Sellerberg (1978).
3. For a discussion, see Burns (1955) on "cliques"
   and "cabals" as a social protection not only in
   an instrumental sense, but also as possibilities
   for intimacy and spontaneous actions.
4. See Irwin's (1970) description of "styles of
   doing all right", for similar conclusions.

Chapter 10.

1. Shover (1971).
2. Cf. Cohen (1955) and Cloward and Ohlin (1960).
3. Gary Becker (1968) is the first who made an
   attempt to apply modern economic analysis to
   crime. For a general article dealing with this
   area see Warren (1978) and Nettler (1978: 172-
   205).
4. Mack (1972).

5. Matza (1967).
6. Several criminologists have pointed out that kicks and thrills are important motivating factors for juvenile delinquents (Thrasher 1927; Matza 1961; Prus and Irini (1980). Shover (1971) has argued the same for adult criminals.
7. Cf. Pryce, who sees the importance of being in control for the West Indian hustlers in England when he studied their local scene:
   The hustle, for the hustler, makes up for all the intrinsic and extrinsic deprivation of work. Whatever else the hustle might be, judged from the reference position of the dominant society, it is certainly not a deprivation. It restores the hustler's sense of pride and his feeling of mastery and autonomy. He is in control again. (1979: 68)
8. See also Taylor (1984) and Prus and Sharper (1977) where professional criminals are described as spending large sums on different kinds of gambling.
9. I tried to make use of some general questions to measure independence. I did not get very great differences in answers between the inmates and the control group, however. It can generally be stated that the answers to questions that are too broad or general, especially if they are slightly hypothetical, do not differ greatly. This can illustrate the risk one takes if using this type of question, especially when they are directed to groups with such different frames of reference. This of course also implies great difficulties in interpreting the results.
   However, when I used very concrete questions, I got considerable differences between the groups. The question for example, about whether one wanted to be able to leave home without telling one's wife when one was coming back can serve as an example: 62 % of the traditional thieves wanted this type of independence in their relationships while only 18 % of the white collar workers agreed that this was important

(see Table 50). A couple of other questions can also serve as examples of what I interpret as an almost programmatic aspiration for independence among inmates:

"When I am going by car I always fasten the safety belt."

%	Agree	Disagree	No opinion	Sum	N
Inmates	29	58	12	100	(114)
Control group	84	14	3	100	(198)
SIFO	73	23	4	100	(125)

"It does not matter if you do not pay your TV licence."

%	Agree	Disagree	No opinion	Sum	N
Inmates	46	23	31	100	(113)
SIFO	8	84	8	100	(125)

BIBLIOGRAPHY

Adler, P. and Adler, P. 1980. "The Irony of Secrecy in the Drug World." *Urban Life and Culture*, vol. 8: 447-465.

Agar, M. 1980. *The Professional Stranger*. Academic Press: New York.

Akerström, M. - see Persson, M.

Anderson, N. 1961 (1923). *The Hobo - the Sociology of the Homeless Man*. Phoenix Books and University of Chicago Press: Chicago.

Andersson, B.-E. 1982. *Generation efter generation*. Liber: Malmö.

Aubert, V. 1979. *Sociologi: Socialt samspel*. Almquist & Wiksell: Stockholm.

Bannister, D. and Mair, M. 1968. *Evaluation of Personal Constructs*. Academic Press: London and New York.

deBaun, E. 1950. "The Heist - The Theory and Practice of Armed Robbery." *Harper's Magazine*, Feb. vol. 200.

Becker, G. 1968. "Crime and Punishment: An Economic Approach." *Journal of Political Economy*, vol. 76: 493-517.

Becker, H. 1960. "Notes on the Concept of Commitment." *American Journal of Sociology*. vol. LXVI: 32-40.

Becker, H. 1963. *Outsiders*. The Free Press: Glencoe.

Bell, D. 1980. "Crime as An American Way of Life." in *Pleasures of Sociology*, ed. Coser, L. New American Library: New York.

Berger, P. and Luckmann, T. 1972. *The Social Construction of Reality*. Anchor Books: Garden City, New York.

Blumer, H. et al. 1967. *The World of Youthful Drug Use*. School of Criminology, University of California, Berkeley.

Bondeson, U. 1974. *Fången i fångsamhället*. Nordstedts: Malmö.

Bordua, D. 1961. "Delinquent Subcultures: Sociological Interpretations of Gang Delinquency." *Annals of American Academy of Political and Social Science*, vol. 338: 119-136.

Bowers, J. 1967. "Big City Thieves." *Harper's Magazine*, Feb: 50-54.

Bull, J. 1972. *Coming Alive*. Ph.D. Dissertation. Department of Sociology, University of California, Santa Barbara.

Burnham, D. and Burnham, S. 1970. "El Barro's Worst Bloc is not all that Bad." in *Crime in the City*, ed. Glaser, D. Harper and Row: New York.

Burns, T. 1955. "The Reference of Conduct in Small Groups: Cliques and Cabals in Occupational Milieux." *Human Relations*, vol. 7: 467-486.

Calkins, K. 1970. "Time: Perspectives, Marking and Styles of Usage." *Social Problems*. vol. 17: 487-501.

Cavan, S. 1966. *Liquor Licence*. Aldine Pub Co.: Chicago.

Chambliss, B. and King, H. 1972. *Box-Man*. Harper and Row: San Fransisco.

Cicourel, A. 1976. *The Social Organization of Juvenile Justice*. Heinemann: London.

Cloward, R. and Ohlin, L. 1960. *Delinquency and Opportunity*. The Free Press: Glencoe.

Cohen, A. 1955. *Delinquent Boys*. The Free Press: Glencoe.

Coleman, J. 1975. *Addiction, Crime and Abstinence*. Ph.D. Dissertation. Department of Sociology. University of California: Santa Barbara.

Cressey, D. 1953. *Other People's Money*. The Free Press: Glencoe.

Cressey, D. 1972. *Criminal Organization: Its Elementary Forms*. Heinemann: London.

Cressey, D. 1977. *Theft of the Nation*. Harper Torchbooks: New York.

Crookstone, P. 1967. *The Villain*. Jonatan Cape: London.

Crozier, M. and Friedberg, E. 1980. *Actors and Systems*. University of Chicago Press: Chicago.

Downes, D. 1966. *The Delinquent Solution*. Routledge & Kegan Paul: London.

Einstadter, W. 1969. "The Social Organization of Armed Robbery." *Social Problems*, vol. 17: 64-83.

Erskine, H. 1974. "The polls: Causes of Crime." *Public Opinion Quarterly*, vol. 38:288-298.

Fiddle, S. 1967. *Portraits from a Shooting Gallery*. Harper and Row: New York.

Finestone, H. 1969. "Cats, Kicks and Color." in *Delinquency, Crime and Social Process*, ed. Cressey, D. and Ward, D. Harper and Row: New York.

Gans, H. 1962. *The Urban Villagers*. The Free Press: Glencoe.

Gibbons, D. 1968. *Society, Crime and Criminal Careers*. Prentice-Hall: Englewood Cliffs, N.J.

Glaser, D. 1964. *The Effectiveness of a Prison and Parole System*. Bobbs-Merrill: New York.

Goddard, D. 1980. *Easy Money*. Granada Pub. Co.: London.

Goffman, E. 1959. *Presentation of Self in Everyday Life*. Anchor Books: Garden City, New York.

Goffman, E. 1961. *Asylums*. Anchor Books: Garden City, New York.

Goffman, E. 1966. *Behavior in Public Places*. The Free Press: New York.

Goffman, E. 1967. *Interaction Ritual*. Doubleday & Co.: New York.

Goffman, E. 1969. *Where the Action Is*. Allen Lane, The Penguin Press: London.

Goffman, E. 1970. *Strategic Interaction*. Basil Blackwell: Oxford.

Goffman, E. 1972. *Relations in Public*. Harper Torchbooks: New York.

Goldberg, T. 1973. *The Heads of Stockholm*. Department of Sociology. University of Uppsala: Uppsala.

Goldthorpe, J. 1968. *The Affluent Worker: Industrial attitudes and behaviour*. Cambridge University Press: Cambridge.

Goode, W. 1978. *The Celebration of Heroes – Prestige as a Control System*. University of California Press: Los Angeles.

Gould, L. et al. 1968. *Crime as a Profession*. Washington D.C. U.S. Department of Justice, Office of Law Enforcement Assistance.

deGrazia, S. 1964. *On Time, Work and Leisure*. Doubleday: Garden City, New York.

Hall, E. 1959. *The Silent Language*. Doubleday & Co.: Garden City, New York.

Hapgood, H. 1903. *The Autobiography of a Thief*. Fox Duffield: New York.

Hindelang, M. 1970. "The Commitment of Delinquents to Their Misdeeds: Do Delinquents Drift?", *Social Problems*, vol. 17: 502-509.

Hirschi, T. 1969. *Causes of Delinquency*. University of California Press: Berkeley and Los Angeles.

Holzman, H. 1979. *The Persistent Offender and the Concept of Professional Criminality*. Ph.D. Dissertation. University of Maryland.

Horton, J. 1977. "Time and Cool People." in *Deviant Lifestyles*, ed. Henslin, Transaction Books: New Brunswick, N.J. pp.59-72.

Howell, J. 1973. *Hard Living on Clay Street*. Anchor Books: Garden City, New York.

Inciardi, J. 1974. "Vocational Crime." in *Handbook of Criminology*, ed. Glaser, D. Rand McNelly: Chicago, pp. 299-402.

Inciardi, J. 1975. *Careers in Crime*. Rand McNelly: Chicago.

Irwin, J. and Cressey, D. 1962. "Thieves, Convicts and the Inmate Culture." *Social Problems*, vol.

Irwin, J. 1970. *The Felon*. Prentice Hall: New Jersey.

Irwin, J. 1972. "Participant Observations of Criminals." in *Research in Deviance*, ed. Douglas, J. Random House: New York. pp. 117-138.

Irwin, J. 1980. *Prisons in Turmoil*. Little, Brown and Co.: Boston and Toronto.

Jackson, B. 1969. *Outside the Law: A Thief's Primer*. Transaction Books: New Brunswick, N.J.

Jackson, B. 1972. *In the Life*. Holt, Rinehart and Winston: New York.

Kellner, H. and Berger, P. 1981. *Sociology Reinterpreted*. Doubleday: Garden City, New York.

Klein, J. and Montague, M. 1977. *Check Forgers*. Lexington Books: Lexington, Mass.

Klockars, C. 1974. *The Professional Fence*. The Free Press: New York.

Komarovsky, M. 1947. "Cultural Contradiction and Sex Roles." *American Journal of Sociology*, pp. 186-188.

Letkemann, P. 1973. *Crime as Work*. Prentice-Hall: Englewood Cliffs, N.J.

Lemert, E. 1951. *Social Pathology*. McGraw Hill: New York.

Lemert, E. 1964. "The Behavior of the Systematic Check Forger." in *The Other Side*, ed. Becker, H. The Free Press: New York. pp. 211-225.

Lewin, K. 1948. "Time-Perspectives and Morale." in *Resolving Social Conflict*. Harper and Row: New York. pp. 103-124.

Lewis, M. 1970. "Structural Deviance and Normative Conformity." in *Crime in the City*, ed. Glaser, D. Harper and Row: New York.

Liebow, H. 1967. *Tally's Corner*. Little, Brown and Co.: Boston.

Lindesmith, A. 1947. *Opiate Addiction*. Principia Press: Bloomington.

Lofland, J. 1969. *Deviance and Identity*. Prentice-Hall: Englewood Cliffs, N.J.

Lofland, J. 1976. *Doing Social Life*. John Wiley and

Lukes, S. 1973. *Individualism*. Basil Blackwell: London.

Lyman, S. and Scott, M. 1980. "Coolness in Everyday Life." in *The Meaning of Sociology: A Reader*, ed. Charon, J. Alfred Publ. Co.: Sherman Oaks, California.

Mack, J. 1972. "The Able Criminal." *British Journal of Criminology*, vol. 12: 44-54.

McCorkle, L. and Korn, R. 1954. "Prison in Transformation: Resocialization Within Walls." *Annals of American Academy of Political and Social Science*, vol. 293: 88-98.

McIntosh, M. 1971. "Changes in the Organization of Thieving." in *Images of Deviance* ed. Cohen, S. Penguin: Harmondsworth.

MacIsaacs, J. 1968. *Half the Fun Was Getting There*. Prentice-Hall: Englewood Cliffs, N.J.

McKenna Jr, J. 1972. *An Empirical Testing of a Typology of Adult Criminal Behavior*. Ph.D. Dissertation. University of Notre Dame. Indiana.

MacKenzie, D. 1955. *Occupation: Thief*. Bobbs-Merrill: New York.

MacKenzie, N. 1967. *Secret Societies*. Collier Books: New York.

Manocchio, A. and Dunn, J. 1970. *The Time-Game - Two Views of a Prison*. Delta Book: New York.

Maquire, M. 1982. *Burglary in a Dwelling*. Heinemann: London.

Martin, J. 1952. *My Life In Crime*. Harper and Brothers: New York.

Matza, D. and Sykes, G. 1961. "Juvenile Delinquency and Subterranean Values." *American Sociological Review*, vol. 26: 712-719.

Matza, D. 1967. *Delinquency and Drift*. Wiley: New York.

Matza, D. 1969. *Becoming Deviant*. Prentice-Hall: New Jersey.

Maurer, D. 1955. *Whiz Mob*. Publication of the American Dialect Society: Gainesville, Florida.

Maurer, D. 1962. *The Big Con*. New American Library

Merton, R. 1957. *Social Theory and Social Structure.* The Free Press: Glencoe, Illinois.

Miller, G. 1978. *Odd Jobs.* Prentice-Hall: Englewood Cliffs, N.J.

Miller, G. 1980. "Non-Occupational Work." *Social Problems,* vol. 27: 381-391.

Miller, W. 1958. "Lower Class Culture as a Generating Milieu of Gang Delinquency." *Journal of Social Issues,* vol. 14: 5-19.

Milner, R. and Milner, C. 1972. *Black Players.* Little, Brown and Co.: Boston and Toronto.

Moore, W. 1963. *Man, Time and Society.* John Wiley and Sons: New York.

Nelkin, D. 1970. *On the Season: Aspects of the Migrant Labor System.* Humphrey Press: New York.

Nettler, G. 1972. "Shifting the Load." *American Behavioral Scientist,* vol. 15: 361-379.

Nettler, G. 1978. *Explaining Crime.* McGraw-Hill: New York.

Nisbet, R. 1970. *The Social Bond.* Alfred A. Knopf: New York.

Ødegaard, Ø. 1941. *Unge Tilbakefallsforbrytere.* Norske videskaps-akademi: Oslo.

Park, R. 1964 (1950). *Race and Culture.* The Free Press: New York.

Parker, T. and Allerton, R. 1962. *The Courage of His Convictions.* Hutchinson: London.

Pepper, A. 1979. *Straight Life.* Schirmar Books: New York.

Persson, M. 1977. *Vissa aspekter på den illegala ekonomiska marknaden.* Sociologiska institutionen, Lund.

Persson, M. 1978. *Aspekter på dagens tillgrepps- och narkotikabrottslingar.* Sociologiska institutionen, Lund.

Persson, M. 1980. *Barn, ungdomars och deras föräldrars syn på framtiden.* Sociologiska institutionen, Lund.

Persson, M. 1981 a). *Avvikande delkulturer - en teoretisk och empirisk granskning.* Brottsförebyggande rådet, rapport 1981:3, Stockholm.

Persson, M. 1981 b). "Time-Perspective amongst Criminals." *Acta Sociologica*, vol. 24: 149-165.

Persson, R. och Dahlgren, A. 1975. *Ungdomens fritid och samhällssyn*. Prisma: Lund.

Piliavin, I. and Briar, S. 1964. "Police Encounters with Juveniles." *American Journal of Sociology*, vol 70: 206-214.

Plate, T. 1975. *Crime Pays!*. Simon and Schuster: New York.

Polsky, N. 1969. *Hustlers, Beats and Others*. Anchor Books: New York.

Preble, E. and Casey, J. 1969. "Taking Care of Business - the Heroin User's Life on the Street." *International Journal of the Addictions*, vol. 4: 1-24.

Proctor, M. 1971. "The Habit." *International Journal of the Addictions*, vol. 6: 5-18.

Prus, R. and Sharper, B. 1977. *Road Hustlers*. Lexington Books: Lexington.

Prus, R. and Vassilakopoulos, S. 1979. "Desk Clerks and Hookers." *Urban Life*, vol. 8: 52-71.

Prus, R. and Irini, S. 1980. *Hookers, Rounders & Desk Clerks*. Gage: Toronto.

Pryce, K. 1979. *Endless Pressure*. Penguin Books: Harmondsworth.

Read, P. 1979. *The Train Robbers*. Avon: New York.

Roebuck, J. and Johnson, R. 1962. "The Jack-of-All-Trades Offenders." *Crime and Delinquency*, vol. 8, no. 2.

Roebuck, J. 1967. *Criminal Typology*. Charles & Thomas Publ.: Springfield, Illinois.

Sarnecki, J. 1982. *Brottslighet och kamratrelationer*. Brottsförebyggande rådet: Stockholm. Rapport 1982:5.

Scheff, T. 1979. *Being Mentally Ill*. Aldine Publ. Co.: New York.

Schwartz, B. 1975. *Queuing and Waiting*. University of Chicago Press: Chicago.

Sellerberg, A.-M. 1978. *Konsumtionens Sociologi*. Esselte: Lund.

Sellerberg, A.-M. 1982. "On Modern Confidence." *Acta Sociologica*, vol. 25: 39-48.

Shibutani, T. 1961. *Society and Personality*. Prentice-Hall: Englewood Cliffs, N.J.

Shils, E. 1981. *Tradition*. Faber and Faber: Boston.

Short, Jr. J. and Strodtbeck, F. 1965. *Group Process and Gang Delinquency*. University of Chicago Press: Chicago.

Shover, N. 1971. *Burglary as an Occupation*, Ph.D. Dissertation. Department of Sociology, University of Illinois. Urbana, Ill.

Shover, N. 1972. "Structures and Careers in Burglary." *Journal of Criminal Law, Criminology, and Police Science*, vol. 63: 540-549.

Simmel, G. 1964. *The Sociology of George Simmel*. ed. Wolff, K. Free Press: New York.

Simmel, G. 1971. *On Individuality and Social Forms*. ed. Levine, D. University of Chicago Press: Chicago.

Sklar, R. 1977. "Franchises and Independence." *Urban Life and Culture*, vol. 6: 33-52.

Sorokin, P. 1943. *Sociocultural Causality, Space and Time*. Due University Press: Curkhan.

Sowell, T. 1980. *Knowledge and Decision*. Basic Books: New York.

Spradley, J. 1970. *You Owe Yourself a Drunk*. Little, Brown and Co.: Boston.

Stone, G. 1959. *Clothing and Social Relations*, Ph.D. Dissertation. Department of Sociology, University of Chicago. Chicago.

Stonequist, E. 1937. *The Marginal Man*. Charles Scribner's Sons: New York.

Sutherland, E. 1958 (1937). *The Professional Thief*. University of Chicago Press: Chicago.

Sutherland, E. and Cressey, D. 1978. *Criminology*. J.B. Dippincott Co.: Philadelphia.

Sutter, A. 1969. "Worlds of Drug Use on the Street Scene." in *Delinquency, Crime and Social Process*, ed. Cressey, D. and Ward, D. Harper and Row: New York. pp. 802-829.

Sutter, A. 1972. "Playing a Cold Game: Phases of a Ghetto Career." *Urban Life and Culture*, April: 77-91.

Suttles, G. 1968.   *The Social Order of the Slum.* University of Chicago Press: Chicago.

Sykes, G. and Matza, D. 1957. "Techniques of Neutralization." *American Sociological Review,* vol. 22: 667-670.

Taylor, I., Walton, P. and Young, J. 1973. *The New Criminology* Routledge: London.

Taylor, L. 1971. *Deviance and Society.* Michael Joseph: London.

Taylor, L. 1982. "Getting to Meet the Professionals." *New Society,* vol. 62: 203-205.

Taylor, L. 1984. *In the Underworld.* Basil Blackwell: London.

Tham, H. 1979. *Brottslighet och levnadsnivå.* Akademisk avhandling. Liber: Stockholm.

Thrasher, F. 1966 (1927). *The Gang.* University of Chicago Press: Chicago.

Trommsdorff, G. and Lamm, H. 1980. "Future Orientation of Institutionalized and Non-Institutionalized Delinquents and Non-Delinquents." *European Journal of Social Psychology.* vol 10: 247-278.

Waldorf, D. 1973. *Careers in Dope.* Prentice-Hall: Englewood Cliffs, N.J.

Walker, N. 1977. *Behavior and Misbehavior-Explanations and non-explanations.* Basil Blackwell: Oxford.

Warner, S., Wellman, D. and Weitzman, L. 1973. "The Hero, the Sambo and the Operator." *Urban Life and Culture,* vol. 2: 53-84.

Warren, E. Jr. 1978. "The Economic Approach to Crime." *Canadian Journal of Criminology,* vol. 20: 437-449.

Weber, M. 1978. *Economy and Society.* ed. Roth, G. and Wittich, C. University of California Press: Los Angeles.

Veblen, T. 1912. *The Theory of the Leisure Class.* MacMillan: New York.

Werthman, C. 1969. "Delinquency and Moral Character." in *Delinquency, Crime and Social Process,* ed. Cressey, D. and Ward, D. Harper and Row: New York. pp. 613-632.

West, D. and Farrington, D. 1977. *The Delinquent Way of Life*. Heinemann: London.

West, D. 1982. *Delinquency. Its Roots, Careers and Prospects*. Heinemann: London.

West, W. 1974. *Serious Thieves — Lower Class Adolescent Males in a Short-Term Deviant Occupation*. Ph.D. Dissertation. Northwestern University.

Whyte, W.H. 1956. *The Organization Man*. Doubleday Anchor Books: New York.

Whyte, W.H. 1956. "Budgetism: Opiate of the Middle Classes." *Fortune*, vol. 53: 133.

Williamson, H. 1965. *Hustler!*. ed. Keiser, L. Doubleday: New York.

Zerubavel, E. 1979. "Private Time and Public Time." *Social Forces*, vol. 58: 38–58.

Zerubavel, E. 1982. "Personal Information and Social Life." *Symbolic Interaction*, vol. 5: 97–109.

Zetterberg, H. 1966. "On Motivation." in *Sociological Theories in Progress*, ed. Berger, J. et al. Houghton Mifflin Co.: Boston.

Zetterberg. H. 1977. *Arbete, livsstil och Motivation*. SIFO/SACO skriftserie nr. 1: Stockholm.

Zola, I. 1964. "Observations on Gambling in a Lower-Class Setting." in *The Other Side*, ed. Becker, H. The Free Press: New York.

INDEX